Real
christianity

embrace the grace,

endure the struggle,

enjoy the relationship

Joe—My PRAYER IS THAT YOU WILL GROW IN THE GRACE AND KNOWLEDGE OF THE LORD JESUS

CARY SCHMIDT

First published in 2014 by Striving Together Publications, a ministry of Lancaster Baptist Church, Lancaster, CA 93535. Striving Together Publications is committed to providing tried, trusted, and proven books that will further equip local churches to carry out the Great Commission. Your comments and suggestions are valued.

Striving Together Publications
4020 E. Lancaster Blvd.
Lancaster, CA 93535
800.201.7748

Cover design by Andrew Jones
Layout by Craig Parker
Special thanks to our proofreaders

The author and publication team have given every effort to give proper credit to quotes and thoughts that are not original with the author. It is not our intent to claim originality with any quote or thought that could not readily be tied to an original source.

ISBN 978-1-59894-260-6

Printed in the United States of America

Dedication

To the joyful Christians of Emmanuel Baptist
Church and the many growing new Christians God
has added to our family!

Thank you for growing with us in helping others
meet Jesus personally.

Dana and I love you!

Contents

Acknowledgements   VII

Introduction   IX

Part One—**Real Christianity**

One—Convoluted Christianity   3

Two—The Real Jesus   9

Three—The First Real Christians   27

Part Two—**Real Gospel**

Four—Relationship—Not Religion   45

Five—Reducing Sin   63

Six—Reducing Grace   77

Part Three—**Real Renewal**

Seven—Newborn   95

Eight—New Life, Old Flesh   113

Nine—The Struggle Within   129

Ten—Game Plan   149

Part Four—**Real Hope**

Eleven—Failing Forward   169

Twelve—Comeback Kids   183

Thirteen—Growth Points   195

Conclusion—Happy Ending   211

Acknowledgements

Every book is a group effort! I'm thankful for a wonderful team of people who believed in this project enough to invest their time and energy into it.

First, I thank the Lord Jesus for His unfolding work of grace in my life. Describing that work in words is a challenging effort. He is much better than words could ever describe!

Second, I thank Dana for being a loving companion and best friend in this faith adventure called life! Thank you for putting up with a husband who pastors and writes. Thank you for believing in and owning God's call on our lives. You are simply amazing!

Third, I thank my children, Lance and Hillary, Larry, and Haylee, for being patient and loving with me in the writing process. During the long evening hours of writing, my brain is often fully engaged and "unavailable." They endured those hours with loving tolerance and understanding support. I love all of you more than words can describe.

Fourth, I thank the early readers: my Dad (Lance Schmidt), Amy Hunt, Bill Bechter, Mary Jane Mason, Judy Bengtson, Sharon Wood, Monica Bass, Amanda Linder, and Sarah Browning for pre-reading and editing the early, rough manuscript. There's no other word for it than "torture." Thank you for taking what was very rough and making it more readable. Thank you for nudging me to continue and encouraging me along the way.

Fifth, I thank Pastor Paul Chappell and the Striving Together Publications team for your partnership in ministry and for extending to me the opportunity to be a part. Thank you to Craig Parker for your great layout skills and to Andrew Jones for your excellent design skills. Thank you to all the team of proofreaders who meticulously worked on the final draft.

Sixth, I thank a host of godly influences in my life over the past thirty-seven years since I trusted Christ and began growing in God's grace. God has saturated my life with great thinkers, pastors, authors, and leaders who have influenced my understanding of God's Word and God's grace on a daily basis. Their influence and wisdom is literally on every page of this book. Truly none of these thoughts are original with me—they were taught to me over a lifetime by a host of Bible-believing Christians through both their lives and their words. I am forever in their debt.

Finally, thank you reader for picking up this book or for passing it along to a friend. I pray it will encourage you.

Introduction

…we ourselves groan within ourselves, waiting for the adoption, to wit, the redemption of our body.—ROMANS 8:23

The afternoon was wearing on. It was hot. The summer sun was at its peak. The day had already been long—and emotional. She was getting tired, and there was still a long day ahead. Pose after pose, click after click, smile after smile, she worked hard to please the photographer.

Her feet hurt. Her dress was uncomfortable. Her cheeks ached from "having to smile." Her energy waned.

Dizzy. Light-headed. Short of breath. Disoriented. Regroup. Pause. Press on.

Somebody forgot to tell her what hard work it was to "get married!"

She was my future daughter-in-law on her wedding day. My wife and I stood with her parents in the shade, watching the wedding photos from a distance. After eighteen years of friendship, we were cherishing the joy of these long-anticipated moments.

Truly, it was wonderful. It was overwhelmingly perfect, in every way. It was joyous beyond description—a picture of purity and blessing. It was a delightful portrait of God's redemptive love—the groom and his bride. It was everything we hoped and dreamed it would be.

But being the bride had its difficult side. It was exhilaratingly exhausting. Beautifully depleting. Wonderfully wearying. There was a lot of work in waiting. Standing still. Enduring the heat. Putting up with the portraits. Holding the pose. Again, and again.

She needed some rest. A soft chair. Cold water. Fresh fruit. She needed to lean on someone. She needed a break. Being a bride was harder than she had imagined, but being married would be a dream come true— the fulfillment of a lifetime hope!

True love was waiting in temporary toil—bliss wrapped in burden. Hope held up in hardship. Paradise was arrested by pause.

In some sense, I see myself and my Saviour in this picture. Jesus, the perfect Redeemer—the Bride Groom who has prepared a place for me. Me, the waiting bride, wishing He would quickly remove me from this present struggle called "life" and fulfill His ultimate promise of redemption and perfection—eternal hope, Heaven, and freedom from the restraints and discomforts of a sin-sick world and a sin-scarred life.

The mothers rush to her aid. "Sit down for a moment." "Have some water." "Eat some food." A few moments of rest, then, more photos. More standing. More waiting. More enduring.

I could see on her face a wistful hope—a wish that, if possible, the groom would sprout wings and whisk her away—far from the cameras, far from the faces of friends and family, far from the emotional chaos of the wedding day. She just wanted to be with the one she loved and finally free to "live happily ever after."

Between photos, her eyes would wander off with her thoughts. Her heart and mind were already far from it all and in love with him; then another shutter would click, another bulb would flash, another "smile" commanded, jolting her back to the present struggle.

The wedding was still a few hours away. The day was wonderful, but in certain respects, the wait seemed almost unbearable.

So it is to be a real Christian—by grace I am rescued into a redemptive relationship with Jesus, promised an eternity of perfection, but constrained to wait with patience for God's eternal purpose to unfold. In His Word He calls it "groaning"—it's wonderful but difficult.

A Couple of Critical Questions

First, are you a Christian?

I don't mean "are you religious?" I don't mean "do you use the word Christian in some vague, gratuitous, spiritual way?" I mean, when it comes to your eternal destiny—your salvation from the penalty of sin and your hope of eternal life in Heaven—are you trusting in Jesus Christ alone to save you? Do you have a personal relationship with Him?

Or, are you trusting yourself? Your good works? Your church? Your religious behavior or observances? Are you trusting *anything* other than the saving work of Jesus Christ to remove your guilt in sin and give you His righteousness in exchange?

If you are not sure about these questions—then I encourage you to read a small book I wrote entitled *Done*. (This is available as a free Kindle download on amazon.com or as a free PDF or audio book download on strivingtogether.com. It is also available for purchase as a print copy from strivingtogether.com.) Salvation is not a product of religion—it's a gift from God that brings you into a relationship. This appendix will help you clarify what it really means to "be a Christian" before you read on about the Christian life.

Second question. If you are a Christian—*do you really understand and enjoy your Christian life?*

From the first moment of faith until the moment you see Him, it is easy to get off course and lose the delight of being His. Confusion and discouragement abound among Christians. Hopefully this book will help you avoid both.

Somewhere between meeting Jesus and seeing Him face to face, we experience the difficulty of "being a bride." The joy can subtly be replaced with anxiety. The grace can be overshadowed by perceived expectations. The victory in Jesus can be overcome by failure in self.

The journey we call "the Christian life" can swiftly move from being "amazed by unconditional grace" to being "unable to measure up." It moves from being a real relationship to being a rigid religion—a system of behavior modification rather than a walk through life with a personal Saviour. Indeed, God's grace does modify our behavior (as we'll see throughout this book and especially in Chapter 10), but we are prone to make our performance the basis of God's acceptance. We get it all backwards, and, not surprisingly, we become miserable on what is supposed to be a joyful, exciting journey.

Why Read This Book?

Real Christianity is a book with multiple parts—all of which will apply to you differently, depending on where you are on the journey with Jesus. Let's examine where we're headed and how it applies to you:

Part 1—Real Christianity. In this section, we will explore how the term "Christian" has been redefined in recent centuries. We will return to a basic understanding of real Christianity, where it came from, and what it means, as seen in the *Bible*, not merely *tradition*.

Part 2—Real Gospel. In this section, we will explore whether Christianity is a religion or a relationship. Each chapter will help us break away from *traditional religion* as our anchor, and help us return to the biblical concept of a personal relationship with Jesus. This section will lay a fresh foundation, even if you've known Jesus for a long time.

Part 3—Real Renewal. In this section, we will dig deeper into practical, daily Christian living and understand biblical principles that will help us enjoy the journey of walking with Jesus until we see Him face to face.

Part 4—Real Hope. In this section, we will discover what God says about handling our struggles and hardships. We'll see the big picture of where it's all going. We will find out why the Christian life is worth living!

If you are an unbeliever—I pray this book will help you have an "ah-ha" moment when you really understand Christianity. Jesus is worth investigating, and there is a high probability that your perception of Christianity is not biblically accurate.

If you are a new believer—I pray this book will give you a real, biblical understanding of Jesus and your wonderful, growing relationship with Him. It will help you become rooted and grounded in Him and His Word. Your new life in Jesus is going to be fantastic!

If you are a long-time believer—I pray this book will call you back to your first love. I hope it will help you recapture the wonder of knowing Jesus. I encourage you to read the entire book, even the parts that you think don't apply to you, because I often meet Christians who are confused and discouraged in their walk with Christ. Many Christians quit. Perhaps this book will help you avoid that path and stay on the joyful side of the journey.

Would You Like to Enjoy the Journey?

Would you like to *understand* and *enjoy* your Christian life?

That's the central purpose of this book—to help you love Jesus Christ and grow in His Word personally for the rest of your life.

You don't have to be held hostage by misunderstanding or misinformation. With a biblical perspective, you can come to a point of rest, peace, and true joy. You can discover, or rediscover, the joy of your salvation. You can return to the delight of being a "newborn" in God's family.

You were not saved to languish in shame and guilt but to be rescued *from* it! You are the child of a loving Father, the delight of a sovereign Deity who loved you enough to lay down His life for you. *"Greater love hath no man than this, that a man lay down his life for his friends"* (John 15:13).

It's time you discover the joy of simply being a real Christian—being *in Jesus*. It's time to unchain yourself from false expectation and self-incrimination. It's time to recapture the wonderful delight of being *saved by grace.*

I can't teach you how to live the Christian life; only Jesus can do that. Hopefully these pages will help you fall in love with the Saviour—the one who not only saves you from *sin*, but from *yourself*. It is my hope that, by the end of this book, your love for Jesus will grow, and you will grab His hand and never stop walking with Him until you see Him.

No matter how successful (or not) you are at "living the Christian life"—whether you hobble, limp, or leap across your finish line—I pray you will love Him and enjoy Him all the way!

You're Weary, but He's in Love

Being a bride is overwhelmingly wonderful! But there are forces at work in your life that oppose the joy—they work overtime to fuel fear, anxiety, and condemnation. It's easy to descend into discouragement and to fall away from Jesus. It's easy to wander from grace and to find ourselves captive to *lies* and *laws* that drain us of joy and strength.

The journey is long. The day is hot. The wedding seems a long way off, and strength fails. Perhaps you feel like a failure—unfit, undeserving, and unable.

A voice inside your head whispers—*Why would He even want me?*

Perhaps you're disillusioned. Defeated. Despairing.

Truth is—Jesus absolutely loves you. You may have disappointed yourself but not Him. You are weak in yourself, but He's not weak. You may feel faint and wonder why He would care for you. You may fear you will not measure up or please Him.

But He's not measuring you up. He saved you from having to measure up. He fulfilled all the law because you couldn't. In salvation, He gave you *His* righteousness in exchange for *your* sinfulness.

He isn't comparing you to anyone or anything else. You cannot possibly be more perfect in His eyes—no matter what you do. You are His delight. You are His redeemed. You are complete in Him. Period.

It's called *grace.*

In the chapters ahead, we're going to learn a lot about God's grace and the love, faith, and obedience that it develops in our lives. We'll see who Jesus really is and how He transforms our lives from the inside out. We'll see why we struggle and the incredible resource of God's grace to give us victory over the flesh. And we'll see how all along the journey— yes, even in our daily battle with sin—we can enjoy our relationship with our Saviour.

The journey can be depleting. The wait is sheer agony. The struggle is often blinding. It's time to regroup. Catch your breath. Lean a minute. Orient your heart to His Word. Calibrate your identity to Him. There are some critical things you simply *must know* about being a "real Christian." This is different than you expected it to be—harder but better.

Don't give up. Don't sink in discouragement. The wedding is close and your Groom is near. The wait is a lot to bear, but full redemption is real and very soon.

And yes, you can enjoy being a real Christian. Let's find out how!

PART ONE

Real Christianity

One

Convoluted Christianity
How Christianity was Hijacked

Every year, more than ten million Americans are the victims of identity theft. Their names are hijacked by some cyber-savvy, unscrupulous individual.

In 2001, a twenty-year-old named Jerry Phillips hijacked the name of a Connecticut salesman, John Harrison. He opened and maxed out charge accounts with Lowes, Home Depot, Sears, and others. He bought two new cars and two new motorcycles. In just four short months, Harrison had over $265,000 charged against his name—and no easy way to prove it wasn't him! He was guilty until proven innocent.

Harrison invested over two thousand hours of his personal time and thousands of dollars in legal fees to convince authorities he didn't make these purchases. After a lengthy investigation, police finally arrested Phillips for the crime. But sadly, four years later, Harrison was still strapped with $140,000 of debt against his name—regardless of the fact that a justice department letter verified his innocence.

Similarly, Christianity has had an identity theft. The name *Christian* has been hijacked. Millions of people view the term through a phony lens or a skewed perspective.

What Do People Think of "Christianity"?

What do you think of when you hear the word *Christian?*

Survey any cross-section of Americans and you will discover great confusion about the term *Christian.* What does it really mean? What does it represent? How has it been hijacked and redefined in modern culture? And why does this matter?

Few terms are so misunderstood. A centuries-old identity theft has left humanity with great perplexity about the terms *Christian, Christianity,* and *Christ.* Depending on who you're asking, the name *Christian* has been rendered confusing and complicated. With it, the message of Jesus and the Bible has also been skewed and grossly misrepresented.

Culprit #1—Religion Itself

Church structures and powerful denominations have muddied the waters of God's Word and the term *Christian.* Time doesn't permit us to unpack all the wars, the political power struggles, and the man-centered movements that have adopted the banner of "Christian" and misrepresented Jesus. These institutions hold people hostage to manmade traditions, works-based salvation, and complex structures of false teaching. Almost none of it can be found in Jesus' original message!

Nearly every day of my life, I meet people who grew up in a religious structure that was oppressive and confusing. They were raised to believe that the Bible was not understandable or relevant; that God was only reachable through a priest or saint; that Jesus didn't pay for all of our sin; and that keeping laws and traditions is the way of eternal salvation. To them, "Jesus and His way" seems complicated. This is a system that holds people hostage to fear and anxiety—as do most religions.

No matter what it's called, this is not Christian. And you will not find this type of "religion" described in the Bible. It's far removed from the personal and loving relationship that God truly desires to have with you.

Culprit #2—Christianity Itself

Those who claim to know and follow Jesus are often His worst representatives. As Mahatma Gandhi put it, "I'd be a Christian if it were not for the Christians!" If you asked the average person to describe the average Christian you would get something like this:

- A religious person, or someone who goes to church and tries to be good.
- A person who thinks they are better than others—"holier than thou...."
- A person who is judgmental and always evaluating others.
- A person who is hypocritical, or doesn't practice what he preaches.
- A person who is confrontational, pious, and likes to argue.
- A person who is narrow-minded and out of touch with real-life issues.
- A person who is reclusive from people who are not just like him.
- A person who is one-dimensional or only interested in other Christians.

While there may be fragments of truth in this list—it is, in large part, a *caricature* of what the Bible calls "Christian." You could add your own caricatures to this list.

As a Christian, I'm the first to admit, it's much easier to believe in Christianity than to be a Christian. Every Christian struggles to make his behavior match his belief. We all have a tendency to tarnish the name of Jesus. As His children, we don't always accurately represent the family name.

Culprit #3—The Culture

"Christian" caricatures abound. Satan will do everything he can to blind minds and misrepresent God's message. Whether it's a movie, a sitcom, or a bizarre news story, examples abound of so-called "Christian" people doing crazy things in the name of Jesus.

In addition to this, many people co-opt the name. Politicians throw "Christian" into a campaign to grow their voting base. Athletes use "Christian" to advance their career and claim "God's favor" on the field. Businesses claim "Christian" to build customer relationships and feign integrity. "Christian" has become a term of convenience—neatly morphed into a variety of situations to fit the necessary caricature or agenda.

Honestly, "Christian" is one of the most hijacked and misappropriated names in human history. These caricatures overshadow the truth and keep intelligent people from authentically investigating Jesus and His message.

Not every church group or faith-based group that calls itself "Christian" actually is. Not every use of the term is consistent with what the Bible calls "Christian." In fact, many who use the term don't even really understand its meaning.

This all adds up to a very confusing picture of a centuries-old term.

As a side note, to the degree that Christians have a bad name or image because of our actual beliefs in Jesus or His Word, so be it. Not everybody values truth or cares to be intellectually honest with the facts. Authentic Christians find their belief in the Bible as an absolute source of truth—that's a fixed position. But often Christians have a bad name because of behavior and dispositions inconsistent with the character and teaching of Jesus.

Setting Aside Bad Information

There's a very good chance, in the middle of all the cultural noise, that you have bad information about Christianity—even if you claim to be a Christian. You are being sabotaged. Forces are working against you to prevent you from experiencing the joyful Christian journey by God's definition.

Maybe you have ruled out considering Jesus or His message. Maybe you think you know what Christianity is and have therefore rendered it irrelevant to your life. Maybe if I knew what you think of "Christianity"—I wouldn't believe in it *either!* Perhaps you have seen a form of "Christianity" that is a radical distortion of truth.

Wouldn't it be sad to never fully investigate and understand the truth of this man Jesus?

Perhaps you are a Christian who truly knows Jesus personally, but you have been caught on the ladder of works. You're working hard to be better and you're losing hope. Somehow you've lost sight of grace. You've become gripped by spiritual exhaustion, hounded by failure, shamed by guilt. You can't imagine that God is delighted with you.

What if you could be released from all that pressure? What if you have been misinformed? What if there's a Christian walk and relationship entirely different from these experiences and hijacked paradigms?

There is. There's a good chance that you have misinformation about Jesus and His call. What you don't know will hurt you. What you misunderstand will take you down the wrong road. You will become disillusioned, disappointed, and discouraged. Your faulty expectations and theological framework will have a collision with your painful reality, and you will blame God.

Worst case: you will walk away from Him and never experience the relationship He desires. Best case: you will suffer and struggle forward with faulty beliefs and disillusionment, unnecessarily enduring a joyless journey as a Christian.

That doesn't sound like the abundant life that Jesus promised!

Take a trip with me. Let's take a fresh, biblical look at Jesus and His message from the Bible. Let's turn the page and go back to the first century together. Where did this hijacked term "Christian" really come from, what did it mean at its beginning, and why is this so important for us today?

Next stop—first-century Israel.

Two

The Real Jesus
He's a Person, Not a Tradition

God, who at sundry times and in divers manners spake in time past unto the fathers by the prophets, Hath in these last days spoken unto us by his Son, whom he hath appointed heir of all things, by whom also he made the worlds; Who being the brightness of his glory, and the express image of his person, and upholding all things by the word of his power, when he had by himself purged our sins, sat down on the right hand of the Majesty on high;—Hebrews 1:1–3

The scene opens in Israel—Jerusalem to be exact.

The year is about 33 AD. The course of human history is being altered by events that are unfolding. The Roman Empire is ruling this part of the world. The nation of Israel—a people who pride themselves in their national identity as "God's chosen people"—is begrudgingly tolerating Roman occupation. The Roman government is begrudgingly tolerating the Jewish way of life and worship. Jerusalem is a melting pot of ethnicities as a regional center of culture, commerce, and travel.

To make matters worse, Jewish religious politics are complicated. Judaism has morphed into a spiderweb of different sects, each with their own leaders, endless laws, and power struggles. These leaders have greatly augmented their system of religious laws and sacred observances to the point of oppressing the common people of Israel. They have a strong religious strangle-hold on the Jewish population.

Rome wants world dominance. Jewish rulers want control of Israel. Jewish people want freedom from both!

Enter Jesus.

An Unexpected Saviour

Miraculous in His birth, His life, His teaching, His deeds, and in His fulfillment of prophecy, Jesus was no regular man—He was supernatural. He was the one and only eternal God manifested in human flesh.

> *And without controversy great is the mystery of godliness: God was manifest in the flesh, justified in the Spirit, seen of angels, preached unto the Gentiles, believed on in the world, received up into glory.*
> —1 TIMOTHY 3:16

After growing up in relative poverty and obscurity in the home of a carpenter, at age thirty, this penniless, unknown man steps out of a small village onto the pages of human history—like no world leader or personality has ever done. With no formal education, no twenty-first century marketing hype, and no technological resources, this man single-handedly captivates a nation and its surrounding regions.

His teaching was profound. He spoke of God as no man ever had. He knew God's Word like no religious authority ever could. He drew tens of thousands of listeners out of cities and villages all over the region to remote hillsides, where His words held them captivated for hours on end.

And they were astonished at his doctrine: for he taught them as one that had authority, and not as the scribes.—MARK 1:22

His works were powerful. He healed the lame, restored sight to the blind, cured the diseased, and even raised the dead! He performed countless miracles. Word spread like wildfire. If there were an internet, Jesus would have been trending on social networks. Everyone was talking. Everyone wanted to see this man. Everyone wanted to hear Him teach, see Him perform a miracle, or better yet, to be a part of a miracle.

And Jesus went forth, and saw a great multitude, and was moved with compassion toward them, and he healed their sick.—MATTHEW 14:14

His love was incomparable. He broke all the expectations of what a "man from God" or a Messiah would be. Religion would have defined and confined Him to a much different box. He loved the worst that humanity had to offer—the most sinful, the most broken, the most devastated. He accepted those whom society's elite disdained. He spent time with those the religious crowd rejected. He reached out to the morally bankrupt, the lowest of the lowlife, the poorest of the poor of Israel. He identified most with those who had the least to offer Him.

Those who failed miserably at religion were captivated and loved by Jesus. As God, He showed that holiness was not incompatible with compassion, grace, and mercy.

Then drew near unto him all the publicans and sinners for to hear him. And the Pharisees and scribes murmured, saying, This man receiveth sinners, and eateth with them.—LUKE 15:1–2

Now before the feast of the passover, when Jesus knew that his hour was come that he should depart out of this world unto the Father, having loved his own which were in the world, he loved them unto the end.—JOHN 13:1

His claims were confrontational. Jesus defied the status quo with radical verbiage and behavior. He didn't embrace the man-made religious systems of His day—He crushed them. He rebuked the religious leaders for their hypocrisy and legalism. He warned of ladening people with oppressive laws. He rebuked the practice of *"teaching for doctrines the commandments of men"* (Mark 7:7). He broke made-made laws that religious structures valued. He embraced people that religion cast out. He said things that angered and mortified those who claimed to love and serve God.

He was no friend of complicated religious structures and had no semblance of what the religious elite were expecting in a "Messiah" or a Saviour.

He claimed to be God—often! He claimed to forgive sins—freely and with total disregard to religious laws or procedure. He claimed to be the *only* and *exclusive* way to God, the door to salvation, the bread of eternal life. He said no one could come to God except *through Him.*

The real Jesus was outrageous to religion—both then and now!

> *Jesus saith unto him, I am the way, the truth, and the life: no man cometh unto the Father, but by me. Jesus saith unto him, Have I been so long time with you, and yet hast thou not known me, Philip? he that hath seen me hath seen the Father; and how sayest thou then, Shew us the Father?*
> —JOHN 14:6, 9

Jesus was simply a renegade in the eyes of the establishment of the day. This is why they hated Him, plotted against Him, and finally put Him to death.

The Death of the Dream

Just three short years into His public ministry, it all came to an abrupt and bloody halt.

The ruling religious leaders finally "got their man." Through a well-plotted, "under-the-cover-of-darkness" conspiracy, Jesus was captured, beaten, tried, and crucified—quickly and violently. Jews and Romans cooperated in an unlikely alliance. The Jewish public opinion turned on a dime—as if fueled by tabloid mania and social media gossip.

It appeared Jesus was a fraud Messiah, and His beaten, bloody body hanging between two thieves at a busy Jerusalem intersection was proof. It was also proof to all passers-by that Rome would crush all threats and that Judaism would sell its soul to retain control.

For the gawking public, the entertainment value of the spectacle was probably enhanced by the "fate" of a timely earthquake. This was followed by a midday darkness that was eerily coincidental with Jesus' loud cry "IT IS FINISHED!"—and then His final breaths.

Some distance away, on the temple mount, the unthinkable—the unimaginable happened at the same moment. The veil—that sacred drape that symbolically separated God and man—was torn in two. God indeed had made Himself accessible to all of humanity—as if to say, "Come boldly before Me!" He no longer required a priest or a blood sacrifice or a system of atonement. The atonement had been made by Jesus once and for all.

Priestly mediators were no longer required—for the final High Priest, Jesus, had entered the Heavenly Holy of Holies with a final sacrifice for sins forever. The sacrificial system had been fulfilled once and for all with the final sacrifice of Jesus. The necessary payment—full and final—had been made for the sins of the human race. It is finished. Paid in full.

Jesus' death accomplished what all the world religions, all the sacrifices of all time, all the good works of any man that ever lived, all the moral laws of all societies and civilizations could *never* accomplish. Jesus had atoned for sin—*all sin, forever.* Jesus, the God-man, sacrificed

Himself so that all of humanity could have free access to God—by grace, through faith. Not through goodness. Not through religion. Not through moral laws. Not through behavior-modification. Not through sacrifices or rituals or traditions.

This is why He said, *"…I am the way, the truth, and the life: no man cometh unto the Father, but by me"* (John 14:6).

This is why it says in Hebrews, *"But this man, after he had offered one sacrifice for sins for ever, sat down on the right hand of God"* (Hebrews 10:12).

Crucifixion. Earthquake. Darkness.

Some actually believed in Him—including a Roman centurion at the cross. But for the most part, the crowd dispersed. The show was over. The dream was dead. Jesus was a fraud, Jews were still in bondage, and life under Roman rule would continue for the foreseeable future. Messiah was not. Everybody went back to their regular routines under Roman rule.

Unbelieving Followers

Jesus' followers requested His body, prepared Him for burial, and placed Him in a donated tomb given by a wealthy "secret follower." How they must have grieved as they washed His lifeless corpse. They must have remembered His captivating love, His joyful and gracious personality. They must have replayed His miracles and rehearsed His teachings in their minds. His laughter must have rung in their ears as they folded his lifeless arms and wrapped His limp body in burial cloths. Then they placed Him into the tomb.

Perhaps they *wanted* to believe what He said about going away, raising the temple in three days, and coming back to life. But this was no "hopeful hillside." Those were inspiring speeches and good memories, but this was dark and devastating.

This was a very bloody, present, painful reality. The dream was very much dead.

The conspiracy, however, was very much alive. In the halls of power, the spin doctors were feverishly at work to control the storyline and to craft the narrative in their favor. The rulers needed certainty to squelch this new "Jesus movement." They wanted all credibility unquestionably destroyed. A powerful Roman guard detail at the tomb for three days would suffice. This would discredit Jesus and His followers with absolute finality.

For three days, Rome posted guards at the tomb. Craziness. For three days, Jesus' followers held their breath in hiding, wondering if they would be next for execution. In hiding, they feared the rulers, mourned their loss, and planned their next move. It wasn't supposed to end this way.

By the way—no one *really* expected a resurrection. Least of all, Jesus' followers. They weren't waiting for a resurrection. They were waiting for their own execution.

For Peter (one of Jesus' most loyal disciples)—with "hostile government take-over and national revolution" off the table—it was back to the old life of fishing. During Jesus' trial, Peter had denied that he even knew Christ—not just once, but three times. High hopes of prestige and position in a new kingdom were dashed on the rocks of reality at the foot of a rugged cross. His fantasy of political prestige and a life of power and pleasure had evaporated like frosty breath on a cold morning. Dead dreams were wrapped in the grave clothes of a dead Messiah, sealed in a well-guarded tomb behind a massive stone that wasn't going anywhere.

How much more permanent could this be? How much more irreversible could circumstances appear? Done. Over. Finished. Dead. Not nearly-dead. Not part-dead. All-the-way dead.

But the morning of the third day changed everything!

Where is the Truth?

Another earthquake brought angelic visitors. A giant stone moved. Roman guards were rendered immobile. An angel announced, "Jesus is risen!" A grave cloth lay neatly folded—as though Jesus woke up from a nap and made His bed. A few Jesus-followers frantically shared an angelic message with His other followers—who answered them with a proverbial "shut up."

Two disciples made a frantic sprint to the tomb, only to find an alarming scene and no dead body. Not far away, desperate Roman guards were fabricating a story of being overpowered by stealthy, ninja-like Jesus-followers. No one could make this stuff up.

It was all suddenly overturned and bizarre. Jesus was dead—but now missing—but still presumed dead. Jews and Romans were releasing the "stolen-body story" to save their own hides and to manage public opinion. Disciples were completely flummoxed—not knowing whether to hide, run, mourn, celebrate, or fish. For those first few hours of the third day, everything seemed suspended—the narrative was holding its breath.

Where was the Truth?

One thing is certain, in His resurrected body, He liked walking. Strolling through a garden, He appeared to Mary. That's when she knew the Truth.

He took a walk to Emmaus—engaging in captivating Old Testament theology with unwitting friends, eating a meal as their hearts burned with His words and presence. Then He vanished. That's when they knew the Truth.

Gotta love this one: opting for the sensational rather than predictable, He walked *through walls*, into a room of fearful disciples, seeming to enjoy the idea of catching them by surprise. (Has it ever occurred to you that He could have knocked on the door?) That's when they knew the Truth. Even Thomas the doubter, fell down and said, "My Lord and my God." Jesus accepted those titles, and rightfully so.

Do You Love Me?

Then He took a casual, but, oh, so dramatic stroll along the Galilean seashore in a beautifully convicting re-enactment of Peter's original call.

Fishing wasn't so good that morning. In fact it stunk! They labored all night and caught nothing. Empty nets—sort of like the sum total of your life and mine—lots of stuff, but empty hearts.

"Throw the nets over the other side of the boat!" As if to say, "try it My way," the voice bounced off the watery ripples, dancing in the morning sunlight. That voice sounded familiar. It must have made Peter do a double-take. You know that "deja-vu-all-over-again" feeling. The memories flooded back as soon as the fish flooded into the nets—on the *other* side of the boat. He's been here before. He knows this guy!

That's JESUS!

And that's all it took. Peter didn't even wait for the thought to sink in. Known for acting before thinking, he was in the water and swimming before it all began to wash over him. With every stroke, with every rush of cool water past his face, the tears must have flowed as the memories revived and hope came back to life. Jesus is alive! Jesus came to me! Jesus isn't done with me! Jesus…

The TRUTH—and the DREAM—is STILL ALIVE!

On the shore, Peter pulled himself from the water—unsure whether to hug Jesus or to fall before His feet in worship. Dripping wet with water and discouragement, Peter paused. Somewhere in these moments it hit him afresh—this was the Jesus he had failed. This was the Jesus he had denied and forsaken. Suddenly he wasn't so eager or presumptuous. He paused.

How would this go?

Peter's heart was pounding—not just from the swim. Maybe he should have run (or rowed) the other direction! His head was spinning. His failure was looming large in the moment. But his heart was longing to know why and how hope was alive again *within* him—and *before* him.

Jesus already had a fire prepared with some fish cooking. The boat arrived shortly behind Peter, bringing with it the other disciples and the fish they had caught. Jesus spoke like a man with a plan, ignoring the awkwardness of the moment, "Bring the net with the fish over here." Peter obeyed.

Picture it. Jesus already had a fire. He was already cooking fish. Now, here's Peter—drenched in all his failure, and here's a net filled with more fish—the fish Jesus miraculously placed "on the other side of the boat."

Still, no one dared to address the painfully obvious betrayal and epic failure of this brash but broken "former loyalist." (See Matthew 26:30–75.)

This was awkward.

"Come and eat." Jesus' casual invitation broke the silence with an even more awkward lightness. His tone was almost relaxed. Peter was still hesitant. No one quite knew what to say, so Jesus went easy on them. As men instinctively know to do, they put off the conversation and dug into the grub. It must have been a quiet dinner. Scripture just says they dined and didn't know what to say.

The silence must have been deafening. Imagine awkward chewing noises against a crackling fire. These disciples didn't know if they were blessed or busted. The wait for Jesus to speak must have been agonizing— like kids in the principal's office trying to avoid eye contact. But the look wasn't accusatory or judgmental—which made the silence even more puzzling.

Can you imagine? They watched Him die. Now they are sitting by a fire eating fish with Him. Bizarre. And cool! This Jesus is pretty amazing.

They were, in very silent, personal, intimate ways, experiencing grace—amazing, wonderful, puzzling grace! They expected a lecture. They deserved a tongue lashing. They anticipated a stern rebuke. Instead they faced love, patience, and kindness.

Their thoughts must have bounced between, "Jesus is alive!" "We really let Him down." "Bet He's really disappointed in us." and "Man, this fish is great!"

Finally, Jesus killed the quiet with a single, searching question for Peter.

"Peter, do you love Me more than these?"

These what? My mind's eye can see Jesus nodding and gesturing toward the full net—the morning's catch of 153 net-breaking fish. I can hear Peter's memory echoing with his words, "I'm going fishing…."

Peter must have paused, looked at the net, then back at Jesus. His thoughts—*This surely looks bad. I denied Him. I hid. I went back to fishing. I failed.*

Jesus waited for an answer.

Peter's mind must have raced. He knew this didn't look good. To say "no" would be a lie. To say "yes" seemed so disingenuous. For the first time in a long time, Peter was at a loss for words. He met the end of himself. Finally he spoke, unsure if he even believed *himself*…

"Lord, You know I love You."

"Then feed My lambs." Jesus accepted his answer and unveiled a greater plan.

It didn't sink in. Jesus just invited him into something big—*really* big. Peter didn't get it. He was puzzled. He was expecting something other than grace. He never imagined a call! He really didn't expect Jesus to *believe* him—for his *actions* betrayed his *intentions*.

Again, as though trying to break Peter out of his self-induced guilt trip and spiritual fog, "Peter, do you love Me?" *Jesus* believed in Peter, more than *Peter* did! Jesus saw who Peter was, but He also saw who Peter could be—by His grace.

This time Peter responded, maybe less self-assured, "Lord, You know I love You." In his tone, there's a hint of "but I've failed, and I'm not sure where You're going with this."

"Then feed My sheep." No lecture. No berating. No stern rebuke. Just a question followed by an invitation back and a confident belief in a world-changing call.

Where's the long, stern, talking-to? Where's the parental posture, the proverbial "finger shaking in the face?" Just grace. Recovery. Redemption and reconciliation. No well-deserved dress down—just a second chance. Just rescue, from himself, from his discouragement, from his failure, from his fish-less "old-life." Peter's sin has already dressed him down. He needed a Saviour to pick him back up and put hope back into his future.

An agonizing third time, Jesus pressed, "Peter, *do you love Me?*"

This time with overwhelming sorrow, all pretense gone, all pride swallowed up, all self-effort abolished—"Lord, You know everything… You know I love You." Can you hear him sigh? Can you hear all of his self-effort die? Can you hear his heart speak louder than his actions? Can you see the conflict between his intentions and his decisions?

Inside, he loves Jesus! Outside, it's hard to prove. *Belief* meets *behavior*—and they *disagree*. Belief says one thing, behavior another.

Grace chooses belief and forgives behavior.

Jesus knew the struggle of Peter's belief colliding with his behavior. And rather than berate Peter for bad behavior, He accepted Peter's heart and called Him forward. Amazing!

"Then feed My sheep."

Arms open—Jesus says, "Come back to the call." He accepted Peter's belief and forgave His behavior.

What a Saviour!

This is Jesus. This is grace. This is the heart of God's redemptive plan for you and for all of humanity. This is what I need and you need. Not religion but relationship! Jesus is a Saviour who extends to us an infinite offering of second chances.

Jesus accepts your *belief* and forgives your *behavior*. He gives grace that completely compensates for your failure (past, present, and future), and allows you to begin again with your simple expressed belief (faith) in Him. From that point He invites you into a relationship with Him, following Him, knowing Him, journeying every day through life with Him as your God and Saviour.

The dream was dead and came back to life. The miracle-worker from Galilee showed up in person—physically, bodily, walking, speaking, teaching, eating—*after* His death. The tomb was not just empty. The dead body that was once inside was and still is alive and well—laughing, loving, living, and leading people into a new covenant relationship with God—a new birth of intimacy, friendship, family, grace, acceptance, and adoption.

Jesus is alive and proved it! That proof validates Him as the only Saviour for all mankind for the ages to come.

Jesus—the one who shattered religion with His life, scorned sin with His death, and secured hope with His resurrection—was and is alive to prove Himself as God, Saviour, Redeemer, and Rescuer of humanity.

Jesus conquered the death we deserve, the sin we commit, the failure we face, and the messes we make. And shortly after His resurrection, He showed us exactly what it all meant by going to the one disciple that had *most failed* Him, forgiving him freely and radically, and inviting him into ministry.

Belief trumped behavior! Grace trumped law! Failed performance was overshadowed by humble acknowledgement of love and faith.

Jesus' interaction with Peter on that seashore was a foreshadowing of His interaction with you right now.

Peter was the picture of broken, pathetic humanity—fearful of God, fickle about God, and falling from God in irreversible ways. We are completely powerless to bridge the gap. We've rejected Him, but He's reaching out for us.

Jesus is the Saviour—the one who paid it all on the cross and rose again literally. He is the one who comes to us in the middle of our failure and says, "Love Me, trust Me, follow Me."

There we are, like Peter, dripping wet with our denial, our dysfunction, our discouragement, our disingenuousness. We are completely undeserving and incapable of saving ourselves. There He is, completely victorious over sin, compellingly gracious towards our misery, compassionately calling us into His radical love.

Do You See His Grace Extended to You?

Before we continue forward in this story, pause a moment. Place yourself there on that seashore. You are Peter. You have misunderstood Jesus. You figured Him to be a religious leader, a good man, a philosopher, a politician, or just another historical figure. You marginalized Him. You walked away from Him some time ago. You rendered Him irrelevant to your life.

Or perhaps you accepted Him, tried to follow Him, but failed. Perhaps you gave up on the dream and tossed Him aside. "Been there done that. Jesus let me down. I'm going back to fishing." Perhaps you gave "Christianity" (as you perceived it) a chance and it failed you, so it was back to the old life for you.

Or perhaps you are an ardent follower. Perhaps you are Peter before the denial—self-assured, self-righteous, self-disciplined. You are a hard-working loyalist with whom Jesus should be massively impressed. You are good and you know it. You are mastering the Christian life, presenting God with a stellar daily performance that Christians around you admire and respect.

Perhaps you're laboring for Him diligently, but inside you've lost the wonder of who He is. If you dared to be transparent, you're exhausted, you're weak, you're empty inside—and for all of your law keeping, you know deep within that you still fail. The performing is really a cover. You're on the ladder, climbing hard, but you're running out of strength quickly. You're still trying to save yourself in ways you don't even realize.

Perhaps your original dream is dead, but you wish it weren't. You subconsciously hope there is something more. But you've started to give up hope. The Christianity you embraced is letting you down. You've either walked away or wilted into a zombie-like walk that is something less than intimate and abundant.

What If...

What if you were misinformed? What if your bad information needed to die? Like Peter, what if you're finally at the point for the truth to make sense? What if the end were really just the beginning?

What if Jesus could move from being a historical figure or religious leader to being a God of grace—full of love, delight, and acceptance? What if Jesus, in your heart, could move from being dead to ALIVE? What if Jesus could cover your past, forgive your failures, absolutely compensate for every fault, and fully accept you and love you just as you are? What if He could become your best friend, your most constant companion?

What if He's calling to you in your failure? What if *He* believes in what He can do in you more than *you* believe?

See yourself in Peter. Hear Jesus say, "Do you love Me?!" Hear Him invite you into a relationship—one of rest, closeness, freedom, and trust.

If you have never come to belief, choose to believe. Choose to say, "I do." Choose to say, "Jesus, I believe You are God, I believe You are Saviour, I accept You as *mine*." Choose to move from religion to relationship. Choose to move from behavior to belief.

Get off the ladder and under the cross. Move from climbing to resting. Move from trying to trusting. Then watch Jesus accept your love, forgive your behavior, and call you forward!

He saves everyone who will believe in Him. He answers every salvation prayer with "YES!"

If you will ask Him to save you, He will. All of your sin will be forgiven. All of His righteousness will be yours. All of His acceptance and love will fall upon you, forever.

If you're saved and you've found yourself on the ladder trying to impress Him, earn His grace, or perform for His acceptance—He can save you from that too! He can bring you back into a daily resting relationship where all the *doing* flows from *loving*; all the *serving* flows from *growing* in His grace.

He can bring you into a real relationship that motivates you to grow *with* Him and *in* Him and *through* Him more than *for* Him.

This is Jesus.

He's not a religion or a tradition or a set of laws or standards. He's not a structure of performance or a system of regulations. He is a person. He is an intimate God who loves you in spite of all of the ways you cannot measure up.

Peter didn't measure up. Neither do you. Neither do I. We never will—apart from Him.

Jesus is amazing! To really see Him for who He is, is to truly love Him. To walk with Him through life and begin knowing Him as Saviour, is to love Him more and more every day.

Jesus—He is God. He is alive. He is standing before you. He is waiting for you to set aside all the misinformation and to trust Him for who He really is. He doesn't call you to join a religion. He invites you to be born in Him, loved by Him, saved by His grace.

This is the Christ behind the word "Christian."

...him that cometh to me I will in no wise cast out.—JOHN 6:37

Three

The First Real Christians
Regular People Encounter Radical Truth

Fast forward this script a little. To summarize, Jesus showed Himself alive by *"many infallible proofs"* (Acts 1:3). In other words, "a ton of indisputable data" made His literal resurrection unquestionable and irrefutable. He stayed on earth for forty more days, showing Himself to more than five hundred people on one occasion, and dozens more, time and time again. He prepared and commissioned His followers. He taught them what to do after He was gone. He gave them a mission to fulfill, a love to express, and a hope to hold to.

Then He went back to Heaven.

Peter obeyed. With great courage, he went into Jerusalem and proclaimed a God-man—a Messiah—who came just as He was foretold. He told thousands of listeners that this Jesus was God, that He was crucified for the sins of mankind, and that He rose from the dead literally.

When he finished, he called for repentance. He called people to change their belief about Jesus. He called them to believe and receive Jesus as the Saviour. He called them to repent of their dead religion, their self-dependence, their idolatry; and to turn to the true God, revealed in the person of Jesus Christ.

And they did! Three thousand people chose to believe in Jesus as God, the only risen Saviour who can take away sin. So sincere was their belief that they followed in baptism to publicly proclaim and identify themselves as followers of Jesus Christ. Remember, the Roman authorities and Jewish religious rulers weren't fond of Jesus or His followers. Being baptized could be a death warrant—risky stuff.

It wasn't long before three thousand became eight thousand, which became twelve thousand. Like a raging wildfire, the followers of Jesus set the entire region ablaze with the miraculous, transforming, indisputable news of the risen Jesus. What the politicians and power holders thought they had squelched, suddenly went viral—no, *nuclear*—with undeniable news of a resurrection.

The known world was literally turned upside down (Acts 17:6) with this new "way." The news of a living Jesus leapt forcibly over all ethnic, socio-economic, cultural, religious, and political boundaries.

Roman authorities and Jewish rulers scrambled to stomp out the fires with aggressive action. Oppression and persecution poured out upon the new followers of Jesus. Arrests, false accusations, fake trials, torture, imprisonment, beatings, stoning, beheadings, and more, were meted out with fiery fury and viral publicity.

Would You Die for Your Own Lie?

Seems like these followers would have turned back.

Unless the story was *indisputable*. Unless the evidence was absolutely compelling, this new "Christianity" would have faded into obscurity like a flash in a pan. Like a bottle rocket blazing into extinction, the followers of Jesus would have fizzled and died.

Unless the story was so true, so validated, so *incontrovertible* that it was worth *dying* for.

People don't die for a lie. "Gone fishing" disciples don't randomly assault "Navy SEALS," steal a dead body, make up a ridiculous scam, and then allow themselves to be brutalized and martyred to keep their cover story. Especially not these disciples.

They were already on fishing boats, back in business, just like old times. They had already given up on the dream. Spineless, gutless, and fickle—they had no loyalty to a dead Jesus. Why would they waste time stealing a body, risk fighting professional killers, and fight for a cause that died on a cross?

Why would they go back to a dead Jesus? More so—why would they go back and *die* for a dead Jesus?

Why would so many thousands of people believe? How could so many first-century minds buy into something so impossible? *Unless the evidence was there.* Not a few people died for this story. Tens of thousands did. And many were eyewitnesses of a resurrected Jesus, or knew eyewitnesses of such.

Consider this. As the persecution came to these thousands of early followers, they didn't forsake their story. They didn't turn back to their old way of life. They didn't return to their old beliefs. They fled for their lives—but held on to their faith. Why? Because they *knew* it was true. They *knew* He was the truth. They *knew Him!*

They not only fled for their lives, but they also fueled their faith— they *furthered* the story. Threats couldn't make them shut up. As they fled, they took their news with them—"Jesus rose from the dead! Jesus is the God-man. Jesus paid for sin. Jesus is the only Saviour. Believe in Him. Receive Him. Repent. Change your beliefs about Jesus—about God."

Christianity is more than a "body of beliefs"—it's *a risen body* that leads us to God and His body of truth. It is all about Jesus and what He did. Yes, Christianity has a body of beliefs—but all of that revolves entirely around and rests completely upon a resurrected body and a living Jesus.

This story can't be made up! There are dozens of aspects to the Christian narrative that no fiction writer would have contrived. It's not even in man's capacity to invent a way of salvation that doesn't depend upon man. We want to save ourselves! All of man's religions are about man saving himself. No man would choose to invent this story this way.

No—this is *God's* story. His whole redemptive plan is based upon His exceeding grace and goodness and man's complete inability and destitution.

A Least Likely Jesus-Follower

And as he journeyed, he came near Damascus: and suddenly there shined round about him a light from heaven: And he fell to the earth, and heard a voice saying unto him, Saul, Saul, why persecutest thou me? And he said, Who art thou, Lord? And the Lord said, I am Jesus whom thou persecutest: it is hard for thee to kick against the pricks. And he trembling and astonished said, Lord, what wilt thou have me to do? And the Lord said unto him, Arise, and go into the city, and it shall be told thee what thou must do.—ACTS 9:3–6

As if the story can't get any more intense, another bizarre turn of events ratchets the whole thing up! Remember, Romans and Jews are using all their collective might to stop this message and squelch the spread of this "way." Like zealous extremists, they are aggressively punishing all followers of Jesus. Every time they stomp out one fire, it spreads in fifteen other directions. They are herding cats! It's like they're trying to put the fire out by pouring jet fuel on it.

And then the unthinkable happens…

Their poster child defects! Their terminator turns. Literally, the guy they've contracted as their primary "hit man"—the one terrorist every Christian fears actually *becomes* a Christian. Like I said—*bizarre*.

His name is Saul. He's one of the greatest minds of the first century. He's unbelievably brilliant. He's highly educated and credentialed. He's a dual citizen—Jewish and Roman. He's powerfully respected. He's passionately zealous for Judaism. He's fearlessly loyal. He's incredibly well-connected and religious.

He loves God. And he *hates* Christians.

Think Osama Bin Laden. Think Saddam Hussein. Think Adolph Hitler. Think of any face of evil and then add a few earned PhD's. Saul's face would have been on all the anti-Christian posters and social media of the day. Saul would have been the talking head on the evening news shows, encouraging people to report any followers of "the way" so they could be properly prosecuted and executed. Saul was a blood-thirsty, "Christian exterminator" who believed he was doing God a favor.

How do you convert someone so calloused? How do you get the anti-Jesus poster child to become a Jesus-follower? How do you convince an arch enemy of Jesus to become an ardent follower of Jesus?

Slick story telling? This guy was way too smart for that. Witty scriptural interpretation? Saul knew the Scriptures as well as anyone alive. Tricky sales pitch? He was much too savvy to buy into rhetoric. Kidnap and threaten him? He had the full authority of both Romans and Jews behind him—power was in his corner! Really passionate "Romans Road" presentation? He hadn't written Romans yet!

Get it—this is the *last guy* on planet earth that would ever convert to be a Jesus-follower!

There's only one way you get a guy like Saul to believe. You show him undeniable, irrefutable evidence. You blow him so far away, so pulverize his belief system, so convincingly call his bluff that he could never honestly think the same again.

You prove truth with all intellectual honesty and integrity. You make truth categorical, not sort of, not almost, not "seems likely," not emotional, not convincing, not plausible. Categorical, emphatic, and absolute.

You see, Saul was a lot of things, but he wasn't intellectually dishonest. In all of his pride, arrogance, and zeal, he wasn't so foolishly maniacal that he would continue blindly against irrefutable evidence. He wasn't stupid. He was just absolutely sure this Jesus thing was a hoax and needed to be put down.

To get Saul to believe in Jesus, it's going to take God Himself to rock his world—which is not a problem for God!

The Romans, the soldiers, the Pharisees, the rulers—they didn't want truth. When Truth rolled a stone away, walked out of the grave, and "wowed" the earth for forty days, all they could think of was how to deny it. They didn't *want* to know Him. They flatly rejected what was *obviously* true. They didn't want it to be true. But Saul was different. He was more committed to truth than to politics, power, prestige, and personal agenda. He was zealous and fervent, but not ignorant. He actually *did* love God.

So, when Truth reached out, blinded him, and sat him down—he listened.

Pause. What about you? Are you willing to be intellectually honest? Would you choose a lie just because you *don't want* truth to be true? Don't be silly. Look at the facts.

Jesus showed up, knocked Saul to the ground, and said, "Stop persecuting me!"

In rapid answer, Saul simply said, "Who are You?"

To which Jesus said, "I'm Jesus—the one you're persecuting!"

Saul's instant response, "Lord, what do You want me to do?"

Yep—the worst oppressor of the followers of Jesus became an instant believer. "Lord!" That means, "I believe! You are who You say You are. I repent… I change my belief about who You were… ARE! I believed You were a scam. Now I believe You are the Saviour. I believed You were dead. Now I believe You are alive. I believed You were a liar. Now I believe You are Lord."

All of this happened with instantaneous repentance. How cool. He didn't need to negotiate with Jesus. The moment the truth was undeniable, Saul turned. He wasn't a God rejector; he was a Jesus rejector.

But then came that nuclear moment when God and Jesus were no longer two separate, opposing identities. Suddenly Saul knew truth—God, Jesus—ONE! SAME!

"*Lord!*"

Saul—world's most active killer of Christians—*became a Christian.*

Unthinkable! Unimaginable! Unbelievable!

The Disciples Were First Called Christians

Quite a story, isn't it? *Amazing* doesn't do it justice. *Alarming* might fit—especially if you've never investigated what "Christian" really means. And it's all true. No movie script or screenplay here. No Disney imagineering. This is the real deal.

In short order, Saul (now called Paul) is brought into a church in a city called Antioch. Followers of Jesus have gone all over the region to avoid persecution, but they can't keep quiet about Jesus. They're trying to stay alive, but something else is more important to them. *Truth trumps survival.*

They know a God-man who rose again from the dead, and they can't shut up about Him—even to save their own hides. If they would just keep quiet, the persecution would die down and go away. But they can't. This story is so true, so compelling, so life-transforming, that they *must* tell others—even if it *kills* them.

Now that's compelling. That's belief!

At first, the believers were suspicious of Saul. Who wouldn't be? Followers of Jesus expected that this was a tricky way of getting into their assemblies where he could have them killed. Thankfully Barnabas was Saul's friend. He vouched for him and helped him to be accepted in the church at both Jerusalem and Antioch.

In the church at Antioch, the believers had genuine unity and sincere compassion. This was a truly great church doing a good work, even amidst all the threat of persecution and problems. This church made a massive difference—so much so, that outsiders were talking. Unbelievers were gawking—some curiously, some spitefully. In their homes, in their businesses, about their daily lives, these followers of Jesus were the topic of discussion. This new way was disruptive—disturbing—enough so that it was a pervasive part of the cultural dialogue.

In fact, so pervasive was the presence of this message—a resurrected Jesus, the Christ—so annoyingly present was the power of this love, that culture needed a hashtag. "The way" or "followers of Jesus" or "believers in Jesus" was too long and arduous. Social media needed a shorter tag! So, as culture has a way of doing with epidemic shifts, culture came up with a hashtag for Jesus-followers:

Christians.

Now they which were scattered abroad upon the persecution that arose about Stephen travelled as far as Phenice, and Cyprus, and Antioch, preaching the word to none but unto the Jews only. And some of them were men of Cyprus and Cyrene, which, when they were come to Antioch, spake unto the Grecians, preaching the Lord Jesus. And the hand of the Lord was with them: and a great number believed, and turned unto the Lord.... And it came to pass, that a whole year they assembled themselves with the church, and taught much people. And the disciples were called Christians first in Antioch.—ACTS 11:19–21, 26

The term *Christian* means "follower of Christ" or "like Jesus." It was intended to be derogatory. It was, in many ways, a death-tag—a warrant for imprisonment, persecution, and martyrdom. It was not a compliment. It was not a term of endearment.

No one was using this term to get elected, get business, or get fans. No one would have chosen this tag, unless they truly believed that Jesus rose from the dead. To become a "Christian" was not beneficial for financial, political, or personal gain. Truth is, it was a leap off a cliff—social and cultural suicide.

Jobs would be lost. Relationships would be broken. Homes would be pillaged. Families would be murdered. Businesses would be shut down. Friends would be betrayed. Arrests, torture, imprisonment, and death—all of this and more would be the result of becoming a believer in Jesus.

This must have been some kind of compelling truth!

What Is a Christian?

With all of this beautiful story of brokenness and blessing behind us, what is an accurate definition of "Christian"? Let's lay aside the modern mis-definitions and religious contexts and look simply at the biblical account.

Four key words—*sinner, believer, receiver, follower.*

That's what first-century Christians were. They were regular people who came into contact with irrefutable evidence, a living powerful Jesus, and a message of hope—man can have a personal relationship with God because of Jesus!

A Christian is a sinner. Before you can be a Christian, you must be a broken, sinful person who needs a Saviour. Like Peter. Like Saul. Like every man that ever lived. This may or may not be news, but you are a sinner.

The news of my being a sinner needs to "shut me up"—like it did for Peter. It needs to knock me off my high horse and flat onto my backside before God—like it did Saul. It needs to strip me of all of my self-goodness, self-justification, and self-effort. It needs to flatten me before God as in, "Apart from a miracle, I've got nothing to offer, no hope, and no help before someone so big, so perfect, so holy, and so glorious." It's called humility—desperation.

Until you see yourself in true need of a Saviour, you will never really see Jesus as the Saviour He is. You will always try to impress Him, earn Him, or somehow get to God on your own. In truth, I'm much *smaller* than I want to believe, and Jesus is much *bigger* than I want to believe.

Let the truth sink in for a moment, like it did for Peter and Saul, and me, and every other person who ever came to Him. You are a sinner. The question is, do you realize it, and are you willing to admit it? You can't be a Christian if you don't first need a Saviour.

For all have sinned, and come short of the glory of God;—ROMANS 3:23

Wherefore, as by one man sin entered into the world, and death by sin; and so death passed upon all men, for that all have sinned:
—ROMANS 5:12

A Christian is a believer/receiver of Jesus. A Christian is someone who has come to heart-faith in Jesus Christ as the resurrected God-man. To be a Christian, you must choose to believe that Jesus Christ is God's only answer for your sin—not religion, not a church, not good works, not your best efforts. You must come, like Peter—sinful, failing, needing, and cry "mercy!" God's grace, love, and pardon takes over from there. You must humble yourself as a failure and let God extend His grace as a Saviour. It's a one-way proposition.

You have nothing with which to bargain. You can offer Jesus only one thing—*belief*. He simply asks, "Do you believe in Me?"

> *That whosoever believeth in him should not perish, but have eternal life. For God so loved the world, that he gave his only begotten Son, that whosoever believeth in him should not perish, but have everlasting life.*—JOHN 3:15–16

> *To him give all the prophets witness, that through his name whosoever believeth in him shall receive remission of sins.*—ACTS 10:43

> *But as many as received him, to them gave he power to become the sons of God, even to them that believe on his name:*—JOHN 1:12

> *For with the heart man believeth unto righteousness; and with the mouth confession is made unto salvation.*—ROMANS 10:10

> *For whosoever shall call upon the name of the Lord shall be saved.*—ROMANS 10:13

You don't become a Christian because of your family heritage, your church attendance, your baptism, or your casual mental assent. You become a Christian by personally becoming a believer and receiver of the hope only found in Jesus as Saviour.

Many people think of this as a 50/50 transaction. As though Jesus did His part and you must do your part—He meets you in the middle with salvation. Not true. It's 100 percent Jesus, 0 percent you. Real salvation is when you finally accept that you have 0 percent to offer Jesus, and you accept Him as 100 percent Saviour.

A Christian isn't a good person. A Christian isn't a religious person. A Christian is a broken person who fell down before Jesus and asked for mercy. And Jesus always answers that prayer affirmatively. He always saves anyone who will believe and receive.

A Christian is a follower. A Christian is a person who seeks to follow Jesus in a personal relationship with Him *after* coming to salvation by faith. This is an every day, ongoing relationship that brings growth through the teaching and life of Jesus within you. This is a person that, after being born into a relationship with Jesus, seeks to develop that relationship and know Him personally—like a friend and father.

First-century Christians were called such because of their obvious belief and evident relationship with Christ. They knew Him, and others knew it! They followed Him, and others could see it.

…And the disciples were called Christians first in Antioch.—Acts 11:26

Now when they saw the boldness of Peter and John, and perceived that they were unlearned and ignorant men, they marvelled; and they took knowledge of them, that they had been with Jesus.—Acts 4:13

What Christians Weren't

The biblical account of the term "Christian" shatters a lot of caricatures. It strips away a lot of bad information and faulty paradigms. Here are a few:

These were not necessarily religious people. Some became Christians and were saved from man-made religion. But in the choice to become Christians, they were following a crucified, risen person. They were entering into a relationship with a living Saviour.

They were definitely not good people. The worst kind of people became followers of Jesus. This was not a sect of highly disciplined, social achievers. This was a rag-tag band of messy misfits. Now that's a group where I fit in!

They were not working to be saved. These were not people who believed in "doing a bunch of religious stuff" to be saved from sin. Religion had failed them, and they had failed religion. Performance was something they had given up. They were coming to Jesus empty-handed.

They were not working to stay saved. These were not people working to keep or maintain their standing with God. They were not trying to keep themselves saved. Their salvation was secured by Jesus, in Jesus, forever.

They were not co-opting a favorable term. They would not have chosen the term "Christian" for themselves. They had nothing to gain culturally or socially by being *Christian*. At the same time they had everything to lose—except Jesus! He was all they wanted, and they were willing to risk everything on knowing and loving Jesus.

They were not casually adopting a social tag. Becoming a follower of Jesus wasn't a "try-and-see" thing. We are blessed to have a culture where Christianity is viewed as tolerable or even favorable (at least for now), but this would have been a foreign concept to first-century Christians.

Christianity—Not What Most People Think

The term "Christian" is not what many think it is. If you are not a Christian, I hope you will become one right now by praying and asking Jesus to be your Saviour, trusting Him only for your salvation. If you have made this decision, I hope you will continue following Him in a loving, personal relationship.

I'm not asking you to become religious but to become personally engaged in a growing relationship with Jesus and His followers. Grow in Him. Walk with Him. Talk to Him. Get to know Him.

The chapters ahead will explore the biblical teaching of the Christian relationship with Jesus. There are so many things I can't wait to share with you. If you are a believer, I hope these first chapters have called you back to your first love. If you are not, I hope you are at least listening to God and being intellectually honest enough to keep investigating Jesus. He will have no problem showing you Himself, if you keep an open mind and heart.

I pray the chapters ahead will enlighten your heart, delight your spirit, and cause you to more deeply embrace Jesus personally and walk through life with Him.

To say it simply, there's no way I would still be enjoying my Christian life or walking with Jesus if I didn't know the truths I will share in the coming chapters. I would have quit a very long time ago. Religion would have overwhelmed me to the point of desperation and failure. My faith would have completely collapsed.

The promises and principles ahead have radically changed my life. They will change yours as well.

Off the Ladder and into His Love

There you are (and me) with your net full of fish and your boat in the background. (It's what we call life.) The nets are overflowing with stuff! Stuff you've caught, bought, and successfully stockpiled. Your stuff is your identity, your stability, your security. Your stuff is your life.

Honestly, your stuff is not enough, and you know it. It's empty. It's an old life of trying to redeem or save yourself.

Jesus is all you long for, all you hope for, all you dream of, all the love you could ever desire—wrapped into one crucified, risen, gracious, compassionate Saviour and God. He's everything your heart could desire.

He looks you in the eye. He looks at your net of fish. And then He asks…

"Do you love Me more than these?"

You pause, you look at Him, you look at the fish…

He's alive. He's real!

He awaits your answer.

2

PART TWO

Real Gospel

Four

Relationship—Not Religion
The Impossible Christian Life

For consider him that endured such contradiction of sinners against himself, lest ye be wearied and faint in your minds.—HEBREWS 12:3

For many, the Christian life breaks down because they see it as a *religion* rather than a *relationship*.

Many people believe the Christian life to be a moral code (one of many in the world today)—a system of religion that conforms me to a high standard of ethical behavior. But the fact is, no matter how disciplined you are, no matter how long you study, pray, and work—it will never be enough for the eternal, perfect God. If you started in Genesis and mapped out all the "expectations"—the do's and don'ts of Scripture—you would end up with...well...the whole Bible!

Then, if you focused on doing it all perfectly for the rest of your life, with 100 percent of your effort—you would come to the end of life still broken and failing. Miserably so! (Not to mention you would be absolutely exhausted and disillusioned from trying!)

You'd be better than I am, or the guy down the street, but you would still be proud. You would still struggle with self, sin, faithlessness, and idolatry. You would still be groaning and wrestling your way through this life—like the rest of us.

Compared to God and His holy perfection, our best efforts merely bring us to our knees in utter hopelessness and inability. It all adds up to *"filthy rags"* (Isaiah 64:6).

If the Christian life is a moral code, you can't do it. No one can. It's impossible.

Does that mean we throw our hands up, walk away from God, and abandon any "effort" to honor Jesus in this life? Of course not. Does it mean we are destined to condemnation? Does it mean we really have no hope but to sit down in the mire of failure and get used to it?

No. Both extremes—wrestling your way through or throwing your hands up in despair—would be destructive to your relationship with Jesus.

This simply means we need to adjust our thinking to His Word. Let's recalibrate our expectations and assumptions to truth. We've approached the Bible and relationship with God with some unfounded ideas—that only His Holy Spirit and grace can expose.

It's Not Complicated

Religion complicates things. By "religion" I mean "moral systems." In today's modern vernacular, the word *religion* implies a well-oiled system of climbing to God. It implies structure, performance, self-improvement, and self-discipline that ultimately brings me into a more "favorable" position with God. It's about my *earning* God's approval by getting my act together and behaving well. It's a lot like elementary school. Behave well, get extra recess. Behave badly, go to the principal's office.

Religion is sometimes about behaving well for *God*. Other times it's about behaving well for *others* (e.g., my church, my friends, my social network, my pastor, etc.). Either way it's empty when it's about "my achieving for…" or "my winning approval from…."

This is called *performance-based acceptance*—a tactic that works well in the secular marketplace but completely falls apart in the faith-life with Jesus. These systems have nothing to do with salvation or with gaining or keeping God's love or acceptance.

Sadly, even after salvation, Christians often quickly move from *grace* to *works* in their practical theology. In other words, while we don't trust our "religion" to save us eternally, we do trust our goodness to keep God smiling and to keep Him off our backs. We move subtly from "saving faith" to "working religion"—all to stay out of trouble with God.

The relationship fades—the beauty and wonder of belonging to Jesus becomes a murky, foggy struggle with anxiety and uncertainty—wondering if He's upset, hoping we're impressing Him, trying to measure up. It's exhausting and fear-filled.

At some point in our minds, He moves from being *Saviour* to *Sheriff*. We move from being *accepted* to *accused*. The *relationship* becomes *religion*. *Security* gives way to *sweat*. And the cycle spirals downward into discouragement and resignation—"I quit! I can't do this!" Not fun!

May I encourage you? You're right. You can't do this. But you're not supposed to!

The Christian life is not designed to be so complicated and crushing. *"For God hath not given us the spirit of fear; but of power, and of love, and of a sound mind"* (2 Timothy 1:7). This life with Jesus is supposed to be comforting and hopeful. It is supposed to be upward in grace, not downward in discouragement.

See what Paul wrote to new believers regarding why he sent Timothy to them: *"And sent Timotheus, our brother, and minister of God, and our fellowlabourer in the gospel of Christ, to establish you, and to comfort you concerning your faith"* (1 Thessalonians 3:2).

The apostle was concerned for the Thessalonian believers. He didn't want them to lose the joy or be driven off course by bad information. He wanted them *comforted*—established concerning their faith. That is my heart for you, that God's truth would unburden, comfort, and establish you in your relationship with Jesus.

Relationship—Not Religion

In light of all that we've studied so far, we need to embrace a major "adjustment" in our naturally-assumed theological framework. We need to calibrate our understanding of real Christianity.

When you think of your Christian life, think *relationship,* not *religion*!

You were not saved into a system. You were not saved by a structure. Christianity is not a self-help program.

You were saved by a *Person.* You were introduced to a *Saviour*— precisely because you couldn't save yourself. It's all about knowing Him— walking in close relationship with Him. It's all about loving and being loved by Him. *"That I may know him, and the power of his resurrection, and the fellowship of his sufferings…"* (Philippians 3:10).

You were born into a family. You are called a child, a son. You are sealed by the Holy Spirit, inseparable from God's heart. You were given new life in close fellowship and relationship with an intimate Saviour and Redeemer.

Relationship not religion!

This perspective is critical because it shapes everything else about your Christian experience.

Establishing a Biblical, Theological Framework

Your faith-context is framed by your expectations—what you believe to be true and your expectation of how it works. Your whole Christian experience will be framed through this lens. It's called your "theological framework"—the structure of truths (or assumptions) that hold your faith together. Think of it like the steel structure of a building—everything else hangs on the strength of that steel. If the steel is weak or flawed, the building is doomed.

Sadly, many Christians have built their theological framework with faulty assumptions or expectations—performance-based principles rather than grace-based truth. Their theology—or their understanding of their relationship with God—sums up to "try harder, get better, be more disciplined, and employ greater human effort to meet (or even *exceed*, for those highly presumptuous) the expectations of a perfect, infinite God."

Even a cursory read through the Bible reveals that God *does* give commandments concerning our behavior. He calls us to live a holy life that is a reflection of His work in our hearts. So as we look at a theological framework with which to approach these next few chapters, understand that we're not talking about whether or not we should obey God in our lifestyles. We're talking about *why* we obey, and we're nailing down the fact that our obedience has *nothing* to do with God's acceptance. If you don't have a solid grasp of this biblical truth, the Christian life will be an exercise in frustration and guilt. It eventually collapses when the framework is faulty. This is the reason many Christians walk away from Jesus in discouragement.

The Lens of Religion

If you frame your Christianity through the lens of religion, God will seem distant, impersonal, disconnected from your present pain. Your religion will be like a spiritual ladder that you attempt to climb to get closer to Him, to be more accepted by Him. The higher you climb, the better you feel and the closer you think you are to Him.

Each rung of your ladder will involve self-effort and personal discipline. With each higher step, you will congratulate yourself for being more successful. With every failure, you will berate yourself with shame or guilt. Your conscience will feel better on good days and horrible on bad days. Religion sends you on a never-ending, hopeless journey to climb to God.

Often, after our salvation, we get caught on this ladder trap. It's like we believe that "salvation by grace" is a free pass into Heaven and *onto* the ladder. After salvation, the climbing begins with great intensity, and what an exhausting climb it is, like every other religious structure. It differs only in this sense—rather than working to *win* salvation, I'm working to win approval *after* salvation. Or in some cases, I'm working to *keep* salvation. Neither idea is biblical.

It's a game. The ladder concept is not in the Bible. It's a man-made thing. It makes us feel better about ourselves. It makes us feel measurably successful at being "Christian." It deceives us into thinking we can earn God's acceptance if we try hard enough.

The ladder only temporarily salves the conscience, until it runs its full course—when all of my trying is exhausted and my faults are still real. At that time the ladder becomes a source of guilt and shame, assaulting my conscience with my evident failures.

Another problem with this ideology is that we build our own measuring sticks. We compare to each other by human math and earthly standards. We make God very small, holiness attainable by individual means, and ourselves much bigger than we really are. We live in the belief that our self-achievement really does impress the God who speaks galaxies into existence. It's all a veiled idolatry of self-dependence and self measurement.

Modern religious thought is like a child who has proudly announced that he will build a ladder to the moon. He might become a better ladder builder than the kid next to him—but neither of them is building a ladder to the moon. Our ladders are sad substitutes for intimacy with God. They are props of pride and ignorance that prevent a real relationship with Jesus.

When we get beyond ourselves, and begin to finally comprehend God's majesty and holiness and power, the ladder concept utterly collapses.

I'm not ever getting closer to God on a ladder—not for salvation, not for sanctification, not for security, stability, or acceptance. Not for anything. Ladders are either placebos that make us think we are better than we are or big religious sticks with which we beat ourselves for not measuring up.

The Lens of Relationship

If you frame your Christianity through the lens of relationship—the biblical view—then the truth makes you free. God comes near to you and invites you into a relationship with Him. Jesus becomes a friend offering new life and joy.

The climbing gives way to resting. The frustration gives way to forgiveness. The exhaustion gives way to renewal. The trying gives way to yielding.

God's grace and goodness crushes all my ladders. Grace brings God very near with open arms. The cross of Jesus bridges an immeasurable distance between sinful man and a holy God. With almost reckless abandon,

God invites humanity to approach Him boldly and to be adopted by Him personally. He lavishes unconditional love and acceptance upon all who will believe in Jesus.

> *This is a faithful saying, and worthy of all acceptation, that Christ Jesus came into the world to save sinners; of whom I am chief.*—1 Timothy 1:15

Consider the words God uses to characterize the idea of becoming a Christian. New birth. New life. New creature. Regeneration. Justification. Reconciliation. Remission. Propitiation. Ransom. Salvation. Redemption. Forgiveness. Abba (Daddy).

None of these Bible words imply self-effort or religious ladder-climbing. All of them characterize God coming *to you*, not you climbing to Him. Every word implies God is doing what you cannot. God *rescuing* you. From the moment of your salvation to the moment you arrive in Heaven, you are in "rescue mode"—always dependent, always in the grip of grace, always broken until He completes the work He has begun in you (Philippians 1:6).

Once born into God's family, our Heavenly Father invites us to continue forward in this new, undeserved, extravagant relationship of grace and goodness. He invites us to know Him, love Him, enjoy Him, and yield to Him in grateful obedience. He promises that He will work in us perpetually. He calls us to follow Him and depend upon Him—all without fear or anxiety. This is a relationship of *unconditional acceptance* and *absolute dependence*.

Saved by Grace, Growing by Grit

Perhaps you're grasping this for the first time. Or perhaps this is a reminder of what you've forgotten. For a long time I understood grace in terms of salvation, but I compartmentalized grace. I came to Jesus by grace through faith, but then quickly jumped onto a ladder of my own making and started climbing as hard and as fast as I could to "be godly."

I moved from saving grace to earning goodness. It's as if God saved me *freely*, but then accepted me *conditionally*. I started trying to get my act together "for Him." This was my first step into zombie-Christianity—mindless, relation-less, heartless behavior modification. My primary concern was improving my character over knowing my Saviour.

Does God want to change our character and modify our sinful behavior? Absolutely! Titus 2:11–12 tells us that the grace of God teaches us *"that, denying ungodliness and worldly lusts, we should live soberly, righteously, and godly, in this present world."* But notice, it is the grace of God that leads to changed behavior and holy living, not gritted self-effort. This distinction is vital, and we will continue to see it throughout this book.

The outcome of my self efforts was crippling. God's wonderful unconditional love received at salvation gave way to fear of conditional acceptance. This pressured me every day to *measure up*. I felt compelled to *behave* well in my own strength. I felt stressed to manufacture a transformation—quickly and visibly. I fell under the weight of proving myself worthy both to God and other Christians.

I was saved by grace but growing by grit!

I'm happy to tell you, *it didn't work!* I'm not happy to tell you, I almost quit.

You can't save yourself or sanctify yourself. You can't *grow* yourself or *will* yourself into maturity. Self must die—that's what salvation and grace is all about.

Honestly, we think it's our *duty*. We feel a sense of obligation—deep human indebtedness to such a gracious Saviour. It's in our human psyche—a subconscious, eternal "I owe you" that begins to feverishly hound us—insatiably! We accept our new life as a gift, but then start laboring to deserve it. Not realizing what God's unconditional acceptance really means, we start trying to earn His approval by "being good enough" after the fact.

We move from *relationship* to *religion*, and it's a deathly transition that makes our walk with God tragically obligatory and spiritually numb.

The Christian walk becomes burdensome, futile and, frankly, lonely. It's an exercise in "trying harder, doing more, being better"—only to discover that it's impossible. Like drinking the ocean—with every swallow, there is an ever expanding eternity of waves yet to be gulped. With every decision or spiritual discipline mastered, there are a million more awaiting my self-trip toward spiritual perfection.

Nothing to Offer

Eventually, I realized I couldn't do it. You will, too. Which is exactly where God wants us. *"He must increase, but I must decrease"* (John 3:30). *"Without me ye can do nothing"* (John 15:5). Nothing. That's pretty categorical! Nothing? Really?

Really. Nothing. Your "trying to impress God for your whole life with absolute dedication and persistence" all adds up to a grand total of nothing.

You, in relationship with Jesus, letting Him work His grace in and through you for your whole life all adds up to a grand total of Jesus! It's all about Him. Not me. Not you. We really are nothing. We bring nothing to the table. We can offer nothing but a desperate cry for MERCY!

Good enough doesn't exist—*before* salvation or *after* salvation. I can't be good enough. Good enough is impossible.

There will never be a time—this side of eternity—when you have prayed enough, served enough, repented enough, given enough, witnessed enough, labored enough, worshiped enough, been good enough! This is why *Jesus is enough*!

You will spend your life either trying to "be enough" or trusting that "Jesus is enough"—and your whole Christian life will be built on one of those two premises.

Jesus is truly *Saviour*. Jesus is yours, you are His, and it's all about relationship. He is *enough*. He frees you from the ladder so you can know Him as Saviour. This book is all about how to stop climbing and start enjoying.

Religion complicates it. *Relationship* simplifies it. You were not saved to climb a ladder. You were saved to know a Saviour.

What We Expect from Jesus

Jesus said, "*The thief cometh not, but for to steal, and to kill, and to destroy: I am come that they might have life, and that they might have it more abundantly*" (John 10:10).

Abundant life—Now that's what I hoped for when I met Jesus. Abundant life! Yes, where do I sign up? The problem was, I didn't understand what abundant life was and how it worked. My expectations were flawed. Here are a few of my wrong assumptions of abundant life and the Scriptures I misapplied to form my expectations:

Happiness—Becoming a Christian should make us happy. To me, joy and happiness were the same thing. "*Thou wilt shew me the path of life: in thy presence is fulness of joy; at thy right hand there are pleasures for evermore*" (Psalm 16:11).

Peace—That internal sense of rest and stability. I thought peace was the absence of conflict or struggle. "*And the peace of God, which passeth all understanding, shall keep your hearts and minds through Christ Jesus*" (Philippians 4:7).

Forgiveness—The knowledge that our sin debt has been fully paid. I presumed forgiveness would lead to immediate victory over sin. "*In whom we have redemption through his blood, the forgiveness of sins, according to the riches of his grace*" (Ephesians 1:7).

New life—The magic fix for all of our problems, sins, and hardships. I expected my "new life" to be much easier than my "old life." "*But thanks be to God, which giveth us the victory through our Lord Jesus Christ*" (1 Corinthians 15:57).

I didn't understand that happiness and hardness can co-exist. I failed to see that peace doesn't remove conflict, but rises above it. I didn't know that forgiveness *of* sin didn't remove the struggle *with* sin. My false assumptions set me up for big disappointment with Jesus and Christianity.

What We Really Experience in Jesus

Shortly after salvation, there's a cold awakening to a struggle and to burdens we didn't expect in this "new life" with Jesus. Paul describes this very clearly in his own life in Romans 7:

> *For we know that the law is spiritual: but I am carnal, sold under sin. For that which I do I allow not: for what I would, that do I not; but what I hate, that do I. If then I do that which I would not, I consent unto the law that it is good. Now then it is no more I that do it, but sin that dwelleth in me. For I know that in me (that is, in my flesh,) dwelleth no good thing: for to will is present with me; but how to perform that*

which is good I find not. For the good that I would I do not: but the evil which I would not, that I do.—ROMANS 7:14–19

Think about the conflict he describes. Yes, *every* Christian—you, me, your pastor, the best person you know, and every believer *ever*—experiences this same conflict. It's like Paul is saying, "I can't get my act together! How I *believe* doesn't match how I *behave*. I'm just a wretched man." That's a biblical phrase for *"I'm such a loser!"*

The Christian life is fraught with conflict and tension. We wanted bliss, but we got more burdens. Here are just a few of the paradoxes and uncomfortable realities I experience every day. Maybe you can identify:

Joy + Hardness—Being a Christian is more than hard; it brings with it hardness. It's not always comfortable. It's not always bliss. It's not the paradise for which we hoped—*yet!*

But call to remembrance the former days, in which, after ye were illuminated, ye endured a great fight of afflictions;—HEBREWS 10:32

Peace + Conflict—Not long after following Jesus, the peace of God is clouded by the conflict of struggle. The Holy Spirit, through my conscience, begins convicting me of needed change and growth. Suddenly there's a fight that wasn't there before, and our sin struggles seem to increase.

For the flesh lusteth against the Spirit, and the Spirit against the flesh: and these are contrary the one to the other: so that ye cannot do the things that ye would.—GALATIANS 5:17

Forgiveness + Failure—We try and fail. Then our conscience condemns us. It isn't long before we feel guilt and shame over our sin. Our new birth makes us sensitive to failing, and we become painfully aware of our sinfulness.

> *For the good that I would I do not: but the evil which I would not, that I do.*—Romans 7:19

Answers + More Questions—Becoming a Christian presents me with big answers, but with those answers come new questions! And to many of those questions, God reserves the answer for "later." He doesn't promise to answer all my questions—that's where faith comes in.

> *For now we see through a glass, darkly; but then face to face: now I know in part; but then shall I know even as also I am known.*
> —1 Corinthians 13:12

Does this describe your Christian life? Sure it does. Mine too.

What makes the difference? Where does expectation meet reality? What is the truth that makes us free?

Finding Freedom in Biblical Realities

Look again at the experience of the great Apostle Paul in Romans. This is how he concludes the passage:

> *O wretched man that I am! who shall deliver me from the body of this death? I thank God through Jesus Christ our Lord. So then with the mind I myself serve the law of God; but with the flesh the law of sin.*
> —Romans 7:24–25

To paraphrase—"In myself, I'm wretched. But my deliverance isn't up to me! It is up to God through Jesus. So I can journey on, loving and serving God from my heart, and fighting sin in my flesh, until I see Him."

Saved but *struggling*. Secure but *stumbling*. Accepted but spiritually *awkward!*

After expressing this great dichotomy—the intrinsic spiritual battle—Paul basically says, "I thank God for Jesus!"

Do you see it? "Mercy! I give! I can't! I yield!" This is much bigger than me!

Reality #1—We are saved, but we still struggle.

If you are a struggling Christian, you are a *normal* Christian. We're all in the same boat as the Apostle Paul—it's a lifeboat. We are broken beings, ravaged by a fallen world, stricken with the curse of sin. We've been pulled from the raging waters, unable to save ourselves, unable to sustain ourselves—desperate in every way for forgiveness and spiritual hope. We're journeying *in* safety *to* safety. We're safe, but we haven't arrived on shore. Arrival is certain, but the present is still boisterous and laden with conflict.

Reality #2—We are dependent in every way.

Many Christians see *salvation* as a faith decision, but *spiritual growth* (sanctification) as a do-it-yourself project. As if God said, "I saved you. Now get to work and make something of yourself!" We see God's grace like a delivery truck that dropped off all the supplies we need to work on ourselves. We see Christianity as a self-improvement project for which He provides the raw material.

Not so. We are dependent 100 percent upon Jesus and His grace and power—before salvation, after salvation, and every moment of the journey until we see Him. We are *His* workmanship (Ephesians 2:10). We are His good work (Philippians 1:6). Even our obedient cooperation with the work He does in our lives is a response to His grace. Philippians 2:13 tells us, *"For it is God which worketh in you both to will and to do of his good pleasure."* He provides the resources; He does the work; He gets the glory.

Reality #3—The Christian life is not hard—it's impossible.

The Christian life is not a *try harder* life; it's a *grow further* life. It's a relationship, not a religion. It's a journey you take *with* God, not a climb you do *for* Him. It's an exercise in *knowing* Him, not *winning* Him. If you belong to Jesus, you have *all* of His heart, *all* of His love, *all* of His acceptance, and you *always will*. You could never earn any more than you already have—that's what He calls grace.

Reality #4—We are unconditionally accepted by Jesus.

The Christian life is a relationship of *unconditional acceptance* and *absolute dependence*. It is not only a walk in which you are completely secure and entirely loved, but also a walk in which you are weak, vulnerable, and absolutely dependent upon your Saviour and His strength every step of the way.

Jesus said truth would make you free: *"And ye shall know the truth, and the truth shall make you free"* (John 8:32).

Truth releases you from faulty expectations. It sets you free to be in a relationship, on a journey—struggling, failing, yielding, discovering God's grace anew every day, ever hoping for full and final rescue. And don't worry—it's coming. Final rescue and glorification is God's absolute promise. You're just not there *yet*.

Bottle Rocket Christians

Have you ever seen a bottle rocket? You set the stem into a bottle, light the fuse, wait a few seconds, and…"PSFFFSSPPFFT…"—it sails off into the sky and fizzles with a final, somewhat unimpressive "pop." Short-lived and fleeting—rather unfulfilling. If you're like my sons, you might light a dozen or so at the same time just to kick it up a notch.

During my walk with Jesus, I've met a lot of "bottle-rocket Christians." They light the fuse of salvation, fly off in new faith and effervescent zeal, only to quickly come to the end of themselves and lose hope. They fizzle and fall back to the earth—their hopes dashed, their expectations unmet, their momentary "flash of faith" doused against the harsh realities of real Christian life on Earth. Jesus let them down—or so they think.

What were they expecting? Immediate rescue. Glory. Heaven—*now!* They definitely weren't expecting struggle or hardship. Bottle-rocket Christians quickly discover "I can't do this." But they give up before they arrive at the understanding that "God doesn't expect me to do this by myself!"

In these cases, a real relationship with Jesus barely had a chance.

Choose Relationship over Religion

From the first moment of faith to your very last heartbeat—you need Jesus! You need *relationship* not *religion*. You need a real walk with a living Saviour, not a religious system of reforming works.

Religion leaves you breathless, frustrated, trying harder until you quit. God is far away, arms folded, commanding you to get better. You are nobly pressing forward, alone, anxious, exhausted. Eventually, you stumble. Me, too. We falter under the weight of religion's demands. Well-beaten and too weary to press forward, we resign ourselves to failure. Our accuser tells us we're just big disappointments to God. Failure screams into our conscience—"try harder!" or "you'll never get this!"

Relationship is entirely different. It's the polar opposite. Relationship welcomes you—undeserving—into close connection to God's heart and the warmth of His grace. By birth you are loved. By grace you are forgiven. By God's extravagant goodness and love you are safe in His arms. All of your unrighteousness has been removed. All of Jesus' righteousness has been wrapped around you. You are His child.

All you have to offer Him is a cry for mercy. Utter helplessness. In reply, He picks up all the pieces of your failed attempts at life and religion, tosses them aside, and carries you forward into the irreversible adoption of sons—a secure, comforting relationship. You have nothing to offer Him, yet He gives you all of Himself!

> *But when the fulness of the time was come, God sent forth his Son, made of a woman, made under the law, To redeem them that were under the law, that we might receive the adoption of sons.*—GALATIANS 4:4–5

After all the ladder-climbing fails, God's grace invites me to step off of the ladder and to come under the cross. He invites me to step away from religion and enter into relationship. And everything we will study from this point forward will serve to educate and strengthen us in that wonderful relationship.

If you desire to understand and enjoy real Christianity, never get too far from right here—think *relationship*, not *religion*.

> *But as many as received him, to them gave he power to become the sons of God, even to them that believe on his name:*—JOHN 1:12

Five

Reducing Sin
Reconnecting with the Exceeding Horror of Sin

In September of 2010, my family and I received some news that rocked our world. Cancer! After a few doctors' appointments and tests, my wife and I sat in a doctor's office as he read a CT scan report and told me I had lymphoma cancer in my chest. This was not the news we expected.

Needless to say, it was difficult to process. It was jolting, but it was news I *needed* to hear.

We don't like bad news—even bad news that makes way for good news. So bear with me. We all want to believe we don't need a Saviour. Even after we are saved, we tend to lean toward the "I've got this" posture in the Christian life.

We gravitate toward "I can do this! Jesus saved me, and now that I'm saved, I can do this!" This is an insufficient or ill-informed perspective— I'm still too big, and Jesus is still too small.

Honestly, my wife and I knew something was wrong with me. But we really didn't *want* to know. We hoped to avoid the reality as long as possible. At some point, reality had to be *confronted* so it could be *overcome*.

That's what this chapter is—reality check. This is not a trivial look at little "sin," but a serious gut check. Think of failed Peter standing face to face with the resurrected Jesus. Think of Saul on his backside facing Sovereign Holiness.

Our tendency is to reduce sin. But we need to honestly face the horrific news of our true selves before we can really bask in the endless wonders of redeeming grace.

Sin Is Really Bad News

Cancer is bad news. It's a mystery. No one really knows what causes it, what cures it, or what prevents it. In fact, throughout my cancer battle, and since that time, I have been given thousands of serious, well-intended, passionate words of advice regarding cancer. I've received every kind of cure, prevention, homeopathic treatment, and warning imaginable.

Funny thing is, if I tried to follow even half of it, I would have died a long time ago of starvation, dehydration, malnutrition, and exhaustion. Come to find out—*everything* causes cancer! Seriously, you name it, and I can produce some form of documentation to support the theory.

Processed food causes cancer because of all the preservatives and chemicals. *Organic* food causes cancer because of all the unprocessed bacteria and natural pollutants. *Lack* of exercise causes cancer because of an inactive metabolism. *Exercise* causes cancer because it accelerates cellular activity. *Sugar* causes cancer because it helps cells reproduce more rapidly. *Sugar substitutes* cause cancer because of the chemicals involved.

Tap water causes cancer because it is treated. *Purified water* causes cancer because of the chemicals in the plastic bottles. *Air* causes cancer because of the micro-organisms and germs it carries. Home cleansers, cell phones, radio waves, airport scanners, body wash, and even dental fillings—they all cause cancer!

Basically, if you want to avoid cancer, don't eat, don't drink, don't rest, don't exercise, don't even breathe. You have to die. Death is the only absolute cure and escape from all the things that cause cancer. *Craziness.*

Cancer is tragic because it is an internal *condition* that destroys life. It is hard to detect and cannot be controlled. And it is a condition that can be systemic. In other words, it can infiltrate your whole body at the cellular level. If not contained and destroyed, it will destroy. It's not a sickness from which you can naturally recover with over-the-counter remedies and rest. No, cancer raises the whole "survival" game to a new level!

Cancer cannot really be "cured" in the strictest definition of *cure.* It can be removed (cut out surgically) in some cases, but it can grow back. It can be poisoned (along with the rest of your body), but there's no way to track every cell to know if it's all poisoned or gone. When detected early enough, it can be stopped in some cases. When detected late, it can often be slowed down or "managed."

But in reality, as of this writing, nobody has really figured out a way to categorically cure, prevent, or explain the causes of cancer. We have case studies, and we calculate risk factors. For instance, with my lymphoma, my risk factors included: being a firstborn, being a Caucasian, growing up in a middle-class family, having had mono, having had chicken-pox, and being interested in sports. (Kidding about the sports.) But it seems so random! In other words, we don't know the cause, but being the firstborn makes you "more likely" to have this cancer. Strange.

With cancer, we simply fight it as best we can, trying to figure out what it's going to do next. It's relatively unpredictable. And it's always the enemy of life, health, and longevity. Always.

Sin—A Spiritual Cancer

To really understand *cure* or *deliverance*—we need to make sure we understand sin and its implications.

It seems so trite—and so dogmatic—to say, "I'm a sinner and so are you." While true, that statement somewhat minimizes a very big concept. It reduces sin to solely a behavioral dynamic. It focuses the dialogue on *behavior*, and the immediate assumption in our minds is, if sin is *behavioral*, then the cure or deliverance from sin is also *behavioral*. We immediately gravitate toward saving self by behavior-modification— "If I can change my behavior, I can be free from sin." Wrong. This isn't something that can be tamed or trained like a parrot.

When we think of sin as simply behavioral, we shift our focus to "behaving better." That's noble. That's good for relationships and societal function. It will keep you out of jail. Behaving well is a good thing. But it's also a limited view when it comes to our relationship with Jesus and our deepest spiritual needs.

Here's the problem. Jesus is not a *conditional* Saviour, and the relationship He offers you is not a *conditional,* behaviorally driven relationship. He is interested in far more than merely modifying my behavior. This relationship is deeper. It's *unconditional* and *covenantal*.

We must break out of our reduced view of sin. Sin is not as simple as saying a cuss word, kicking your dog, or hitting your sister. (Although, I doubt hitting your sister is a sin—she probably deserved it.)

Yes, sin *results* in bad behavior, and bad behavior is called "sin." But it's much bigger than mere behavior. It's much more tragic, insidious, and devastating than temporal actions and their short-term negative consequences.

Often, when we think of sin, we think on the scale of "the sniffles" or "a cough or a cold"—something of a minor inconvenience to God and eternity. This is a greatly minimized view.

When you think of sin, think of cancer times billions of billions. Think of global, universal, cosmic, eternal cancer. Think of death and darkness of a magnitude that your mind is incapable of considering— galactic and epic! Think destruction beyond your life, beyond the life of every human that ever lived. Think bigger than the destruction of ten billion nuclear blasts. Think eternal, nuclear holocaust. And then, you're just barely beginning to comprehend the horrible magnitude and devastation of sin and the magnitude of Jesus' *becoming* sin for us.

> *For he hath made him to be sin for us, who knew no sin; that we might be made the righteousness of God in him.*—2 CORINTHIANS 5:21

Our Two Common Responses to Sin

When we see sin as merely behavioral (and somewhat trivial) and we see Jesus as merely a Judge evaluating our behavior, we all have two basic responses. Your response will depend on your temperament and cultural norms.

Our first response is self-defense. In every person that ever lived, there's a strong defense-mechanism. We all want to be "not too bad." We all believe in ourselves and our own goodness. We all see ourselves as "pretty good." We give massive credit to our intentions and motives, and we conveniently excuse our selfish indulgences and decisions.

There's always someone else *worse* than we are, so *comparison* is our savior. Finding someone "worse than I am" makes me immediately justified in my own eyes, hence in God's. "At least I'm not (fill in the blank)." We play a mind game that always ends in our favor—leaving us on the "good" side of God's cosmic evaluation.

Christians, after salvation, *continue* to play this game—comparing ourselves to other Christians, measuring up who's better at performing for God. It never takes long to find someone I'm *out-performing*. There's always someone *underperforming* me. In my mind, this makes me *better* in God's eyes. This gives me reason to proverbially pat myself on the back and say, "Good job! God must really be glad I'm doing more than that guy!" It gives me reason to appreciate *my* effort, *my* church, *my* position, *my* standards, *my* crowd. Creating my own measuring stick and then measuring myself by others always makes me feel better.

It's convenient, but it totally bypasses God's reality, God's standard, and God's position as the only judge.

> *Who art thou that judgest another man's servant? to his own master he standeth or falleth. Yea, he shall be holden up: for God is able to make him stand.*—ROMANS 14:4

(You'll find as we study these principles, the games we play *before* salvation are the same games we tend to play *after* salvation. We pin them with different terms, attach them to growth not grace, but they are essentially the same self-saving strategies in slightly different wrappers.)

We're all very good at defending ourselves, projecting our own goodness, and tipping the scale of comparison in our favor. It's hard-wired into our psyche to believe in our own goodness—even after salvation.

We want God to *need* us more than we *need* Him.

Our second response is self-deprecation. The opposite extreme of self-defense is self-condemnation. It looks outwardly like humility, but it's not even close. It's just another form of self-focus. Depending on your past context, you *could* just bypass self-defense altogether and focus on your failures. It goes like this:

You know you've failed (royally) in life and relationships. You know there is a lot of bad behavior in your past. You know you've violated and offended God's standard of righteousness. You know you don't deserve Him or His goodness. (Me, too!) So you're not up for the self-justification game. You know that's a game. So you opt for a different game—the "beat-myself-to-a-pulp" game.

As a result, you've either given up trying at all, or you've continued to redouble your efforts to "be better, start over, try harder, work smarter, and avoid the mistakes of the past." "God, if you get me out of this, I promise I'll be good!"

Self-deprecation carries over after salvation too. It's a mindset that focuses on self over Saviour and continually wallows in guilt, shame, regret, remorse—as though emotionally beating myself up somehow shows God how grateful and humble I am. It assumes that perpetual remorse somehow scores points with God—like penance. It's subtle, but we attach the ongoing penalty of guilt to our sin. Even though Jesus paid for it all, even though we believe this in theory, we unilaterally decide that's not enough.

No, we must *live* in regret to really *dwell* in the mire of failure. That's spiritual! That helps to compensate. We sentence ourselves to daily languishing in self-condemnation. "I don't *deserve* to be joyful, blessed, or delighted by grace." So we rehearse our failures over and over—and we even call it "conviction."

Don't get me wrong. *Conviction* is a real aspect of the Christian life. But God-prompted conviction leads to confession and forgiveness, not to self-condemnation and despair. The self-deprecating response to sin is a sad replacement for real grace and redemption. Refusing to accept God's sufficient grace and forgiveness is not humble or contrite—it's merely veiled arrogance and idolatry.

You've heard the old line, "I know God's forgiven me, but I can't forgive myself." That's a subtle way of saying, "God, I'm smarter and more just than You, and I refuse to accept Your final estimation of my sin and self. I reject Your full payment and infinite grace. I'm a better judge than You, and I wouldn't let me off the hook so easily—therefore, I sentence *myself!* Since You won't, I will. I'm a better standard-bearer of righteousness; I'm a better evaluator of eternal propitiation; and I'll pay for this my way."

Self-deprecation is not spiritual, biblical, or helpful. It's just a game that prevents Jesus and His grace from being all that you need. It subtly says, "Jesus paid it all, but that still isn't enough."

Self-defense lies and says, "You're not really bad, and sin isn't really a big deal."

Self-deprecation lies and says, "You are so bad that perpetual penance is your only option."

Both are lies that blind you to the gospel of grace.

Conclusions about Sin

Regardless of your response, you would likely agree to some very basic rationale when it comes to sin:

1. You aren't perfect. We're all fundamentally flawed, prone to making mistakes, doing wrong, and failing. We all have a sin condition that keeps us from being flawless.

For there is not a just man upon earth, that doeth good, and sinneth not.—ECCLESIASTES 7:20

Who can say, I have made my heart clean, I am pure from my sin? —PROVERBS 20:9

2. Your imperfection is instinctive. No one ever taught you to be selfish, to lie, or to struggle with negative behavior. It flows freely from your nature as a human being. It's wired into you—and me.

All we like sheep have gone astray; we have turned every one to his own way; and the LORD hath laid on him the iniquity of us all.—ISAIAH 53:6

As it is written, There is none righteous, no, not one: There is none that understandeth, there is none that seeketh after God. They are all gone out of the way, they are together become unprofitable; there is none that doeth good, no, not one.—ROMANS 3:10–12

3. Your imperfections (sins) are harmful. Think about what your sin-prone heart creates. It creates broken relationships, bad decisions, regret, guilt, shame—stuff you look back on and want to reverse. Sin creates hurt—in you and in others—and it forces you to live with its consequences. This is merely the *visible* aspect of sin—"what you can see." Imagine how bad it is beyond your understanding!

But we are all as an unclean thing, and all our righteousnesses are as filthy rags; and we all do fade as a leaf; and our iniquities, like the wind, have taken us away.—ISAIAH 64:6

Then when lust hath conceived, it bringeth forth sin: and sin, when it is finished, bringeth forth death.—JAMES 1:15

4. Your imperfections are more powerful than you. No amount of self-discipline would be enough for you to become perfect. Sin inside of you is *more powerful* than you. It can't be tamed by willpower. No tempering or training, no resolve or rules, no amount of focus or good intentions will remove the struggle. No class or rehab can fix this.

> *For I acknowledge my transgressions: and my sin is ever before me. Against thee, thee only, have I sinned, and done this evil in thy sight: that thou mightest be justified when thou speakest, and be clear when thou judgest. Behold, I was shapen in iniquity; and in sin did my mother conceive me.*—PSALM 51:3–5

You don't have to believe the Bible to understand this. This is just the human condition, but the Bible surely sheds a lot of light on it.

Why does this matter? And why is it important for us to understand?

Religious but Messy

Understanding sin and self is critical to understanding Jesus and grace. It is critical to understanding the relationship He desires to have with you.

Here's the good news. Everything we have concluded about sin, up to this point, is exactly what regular Christians in the New Testament encountered. Very bad people who lived very bad lives came face to face with Jesus, who proceeded to love, accept, embrace, heal, and forgive them freely with no merit, no payback, no benefit to Himself. These were the least deserving of humanity.

In contrast, very religious people who lived very good lives also came face to face with Jesus, who proceeded to say, "Your system isn't doing much for you! You still don't have what it takes. For all of your laws, traditions, systems, and effort—you're still a mess!"

Think of Nicodemus who came to Jesus at night. He was a really *good* man. In fact, he was one of the best. He was well educated, religious, and very well behaved. He had mastered the art of being good. Externally, he was exceptional in every way.

Jesus rattled his world. Jesus got his attention. To Nicodemus, this Jesus fulfilled the prophecies of Messiah but didn't fit the mold that religion had cast for Him. Jesus didn't climb into the box of religion and say "Follow me." In fact, Jesus didn't come to the religious. He came to the broken, outcast, and failing. He came to those who had long since given up on behavior modification. He connected with those who already knew they were "hopelessly bad."

Late one night, Nicodemus approached Jesus in secret, not even knowing what to ask. He only knew he needed to personally encounter Jesus. But Jesus knew his heart and cut through the surface—through the law, through the religion and behaviorism of Judaism, right to the heart.

He basically said, "Nicodemus, you don't have what it takes. With all your goodness, all your religion, all your compartmentalized rule-keeping—you still need to be born again!"

Essentially, "I can't have a relationship with your religion. That's a 'sinful you' trying to make yourself righteous for Me. And that's not how it works. I need a 'new you.' I need you to die, and I need to rebirth you by My Spirit—you must be born again!" Read it…

There was a man of the Pharisees, named Nicodemus, a ruler of the Jews: The same came to Jesus by night, and said unto him, Rabbi, we know that thou art a teacher come from God: for no man can do these miracles that thou doest, except God be with him. Jesus answered and said unto him, Verily, verily, I say unto thee, Except a man be born again, he cannot see the kingdom of God.—JOHN 3:1–3

"Verily, verily" is Jesus' way of saying, "Upon the eternal authority of My Deity, I remove your right to object to what I'm about to say. This is true, whether you want it to be or not, and nothing is ever going to change it."

Jesus exposed the fact that Nicodemus could not modify his own behavior to remove the sin problem. Sin is death, therefore sin requires death, resurrection, and rebirth! Beating sin requires more than treatment. It requires miraculous intervention.

The best of the best in Jesus' day were still so bad, so sinful, so lost that there was only one solution, and it wasn't found in religion. Complete, total, and absolute re-creation was the only option. And humanly speaking, that is impossible!

The idea of a second birth completely flummoxed Nicodemus. Jesus proceeded to explain to a very good, religious man that he was still very sinful, very far from God, and very unable to save himself.

Some Good News

Probably the "best Christian" of the New Testament was Paul. You remember him from chapter 3—Saul. He moved from Christian-killer, to Christian-brother, to Christian-leader in short order. He became the God-inspired transcriptionist of much of the New Testament. He was instrumental in spreading the message of Jesus to the known world of that day. He was epic!

He was also hounded by sin. His struggle with sin was pervasive, relentless, unceasing. It plagued him every day. Early in his ministry he saw himself as the *least of the Apostles*—not bad for a newbie (1 Corinthians 15:9). Later, he saw himself as the *least of all the Christians*—uh oh, he's sliding (Ephesians 3:8). Before his death, years later, he saw himself as the *chief of sinners*—"Houston, we have a problem" (1 Timothy 1:15).

In his Christian journey, Paul experienced a continual down-sizing of self and up-sizing of Jesus and grace. Every spiritual step forward, Jesus became bigger and self became smaller.

Read his heart again in Romans 7, and consider your own struggle:

For I know that in me (that is, in my flesh,) dwelleth no good thing: for to will is present with me; but how to perform that which is good I find not. For the good that I would I do not: but the evil which I would not, that I do. Now if I do that I would not, it is no more I that do it, but sin that dwelleth in me. I find then a law, that, when I would do good, evil is present with me. For I delight in the law of God after the inward man: But I see another law in my members, warring against the law of my mind, and bringing me into captivity to the law of sin which is in my members. O wretched man that I am! who shall deliver me from the body of this death? I thank God through Jesus Christ our Lord. So then with the mind I myself serve the law of God; but with the flesh the law of sin.—ROMANS 7:18–25*

Paul admitted that sin was an everyday battle and failing was an ongoing struggle. He described that evil was present with him, the power of sin was in him, and bad behavior was still hounding him on a regular basis. We will unpack this passage in greater detail soon, but for now, at least see the *struggle*.

Sin continues to be a problem—even after salvation. Flesh (as Scripture calls it) still fights God and growth every step of the way. Wrong still wrenches us and wrestles with us every day from here to eternity. What's Paul's conclusion?

There is deliverance—*gradually* and *eventually*. One day Jesus will ultimately and finally deliver me from my sin-prone self. At that time I will not only be saved from sin's *penalty* and *power*, but from sin's *very presence.* Until then, I can still experience something pretty special, in spite of the sin struggle. Look at it:

> *There is therefore now no condemnation to them which are in Christ Jesus, who walk not after the flesh, but after the Spirit. For the law of the Spirit of life in Christ Jesus hath made me free from the law of sin and death.*—ROMANS 8:1–2

There is "no condemnation" in Christ. There is a relationship of unconditional acceptance, unlimited grace, and infinite second chances.

The salvation and relationship Jesus desires with you is as infinite and unlimited in grace as your sin is infinite in death and destruction. It's the polar opposite of the absolute negative of sin. When the law of sin would condemn you guilty and worthy of eternal death—the law of the Spirit of life in Christ Jesus steps in with a cosmic, nuclear redemptive plan that overcomes all condemnation, all death, all the destruction that sin could ever bring.

This is massive beyond description. No human words could contain the magnitude of this grace.

Sin is exceedingly horrible. It's good for us to understand this. Otherwise, grace becomes small, salvation becomes minimal, and *self* becomes a bigger savior than *Jesus.*

Keep reading, you'll see what I'm talking about.

Six

Reducing Grace

Sin, Me, Jesus, Grace—Off of Our Tiny Scales

When I left the doctor's office on that fateful "cancer diagnosis" day, I had misunderstood something the doctor said. But my wife hadn't. I walked out with a minimal view of my cancer. She walked out with a maximal view of the same cancer.

I'm a pretty optimistic guy, so I walked out of the office thinking positively like, "Well, this is a bummer, but my chances are pretty good, so no biggie!" But my wife on the other hand, buried her head on my chest and wept like this was our last goodbye.

She had heard correctly what I missed. The doctor had stated that I likely had a form of cancer that was less than 30 percent beatable. How I missed this, I do not know—but it was probably a good thing that I did.

I was confused. I had wrongfully underestimated my condition and overestimated my ability to fight it.

So it is with sin. When we think personally about our sin, we tend to *minimize* it, *reduce* it, and somehow make ourselves bigger and better than we really are. This, in turn, makes Jesus and His grace smaller and less "miraculous" than they really are.

Attempting to grasp the magnitude of sin, and hence the amazement of grace, is essential—and even my effort to describe it falls far short.

In reality, sin is worse than you think; you are worse than you think; Jesus is better than you think; and grace is bigger than you think. And I don't mean slightly—I mean by an order of magnitude!

What We Really Need to Know about Sin

If you're feeling pretty hopeless about sin, good. The more hopeless you feel, the smaller you are in your own sight, the bigger Jesus can be, and the greater your hope in Him. The negative must become *exceedingly* negative that God's positive might be *exceedingly* positive.

Sin is a condition not merely a behavior. It's a condition that is systemic, pervasive, negative, and destructive. If sin is merely behavioral, then we will always be trying to manage behavior, and we will always believe that Jesus is more concerned with our behavior than with anything else. Then, life with Him, even *after* salvation, will always be about managing behavior. I will always relate to Him based upon my works, my *doing*, my keeping of His rules. I will always reduce Him to a referee—merely measuring me, keeping score, and judging my behavior in light of His rules.

(Hold on, I can hear your thinking. It's not that He isn't interested in behavior—we'll get to that later. It's that *behavior* isn't the *basis* of the relationship, and generating good behavior is not His *prime objective*. Thousands upon thousands of Christians have crashed and burned in that trap. It's a lie. Making behavior the prime objective of Christianity is a guaranteed dead end in your journey.)

Get it—if Jesus merely wanted you to behave a certain way, there are many other simple solutions than His plan of redemption by death. For instance, He could speak you into obedience. He could think you into absolute submission. Most of creation has no choice but to be or do what He dictates. A rock doesn't resist. It sits still and does exactly what Jesus created it to do—be a rock. In you He placed a free will and the opportunity to have a relationship. He wants to know *you* and fellowship with *you*—this is the joy set before Him, not merely your behavioral conformity.

Behavior is not the *foundation*—it's the *fruit*. It's not the bottom line; it's the *overflow* of the bottom line. Jesus is not a behavior-modification specialist. He's not sitting in Heaven wringing His hands about your tripping up yesterday and fretting over how to fix it. That's a weak Saviour. That's a small cross!

He's a powerful Saviour and an intimate friend who knew everything there is to know about you before the foundation of the world. Knowing Him and having a relationship with Him *will change* my behavior—no doubt. But behavioral change is not what it's all about.

Sin is not just a *doing* problem—it's also a *being* problem.

Sin is death in us. Sin is destruction bound up in our spiritual, genetic make-up. Sin is hard-wired into our human heart. Sin is a rapidly reproducing, spiritual condition at the root level of our spiritual being. Sin resists God, defies His authority, resents His rule, and rebels against His laws. Sin is that which leads us to be our own gods, pursue our own needs, perpetuate our own kingdoms, and please our own desires. Sin replaces God—dethroning Him, and enthroning self. Sin drives us away from God, separates us from Him, and places us at enmity (as enemies) with Him.

> *Wherefore, as by one man sin entered into the world, and death by sin; and so death passed upon all men, for that all have sinned:* —ROMANS 5:12

> *Because the carnal mind is enmity against God: for it is not subject to the law of God, neither indeed can be.* —ROMANS 8:7

Sin is the opposite of God and all that He is. He is perfect love. He is holy, righteous perfection. He is true justice and unchanging authority. Sin is an assault on God and His right to be God. Sin is the absence and rejection of God and all of His goodness.

To make it more personal—sin is in me. Sin is what I'm made of before I come to Jesus—before the new birth. It's woven into every spiritual fiber. It's written into the flesh—the mind, the intellect, the will, the emotions. It's indelibly, irrevocably a part of me. It's an incurable cancer that will ravage and ultimately destroy me. It doesn't need to be treated or managed. It must be destroyed. It must be eradicated absolutely if life is to be preserved.

As of this writing, I've been cancer-free for nearly three years. But really, that's just a best guess. There's no way to know for sure. Cancer could be growing in me right now, even as I write these words. The chemotherapy and radiation were a "best effort" of the professionals, to do the only things they knew, to blast as many of the cancer cells as possible, and to hope they won't grow back. It was a "best hope" scenario, and so far, so good. But there are no absolute guarantees that cancer cells are all dead or that they won't resume reproduction.

Thankfully, that's not God's approach to sin. God isn't guessing at His cure or doing "the best He can" to deal with sin and death. No, God's remedy for the sin condition is irreversible and eternally comprehensive. God didn't deal wistfully, experimentally, or temporarily with sin. He dealt with it ultimately and with finality. That's what Jesus did on the cross for you and me.

We're Worse Than We Think

The Christian life is not an upward journey in making myself better. It's a downward journey in seeing myself for who I really am. And it continues to be that, every single day, from my salvation forward, until I see Jesus.

Don't get me wrong. I truly want to *be better*. But for the life of me, even after thirty-seven years of growing as a Christian, I can't figure out how to *make myself better*. I have yet to conquer pride, selfishness, and flesh. I have yet to gain final victory over temper, emotion, anxiety, and fear.

I've managed to tame and master a few surface behaviors. On Sunday morning, I clean up well like the rest of my church family. My wife dresses me nicely, I smile, I look acceptable, I behave well—but in reality, there's still a lot in me that needs work. Just ask Dana or my kids! For all of my growing, I feel like I'm still a *beginner Christian* in the body of a *career sinner!*

The good behavior isn't a mask or a cover. Not at all. It's not hypocrisy. It's actually my best intention to allow the Spirit of Christ to rule in those moments. It's real, but it's also a struggle, and all too temporal. It's not comprehensive! The visual, external victory is just the tip of the iceberg of internal victories that still need to be won.

Yep, the longer I'm saved, the more familiar I am with my struggles. And for all my years of behavior modification and self-effort—I have rather paltry and pathetic results to show for it. All I really have is a daily renewed awareness that I'm trapped in a sinful body (flesh). I'm hostage to a flesh where the law of sin and death wrestles every day against the law of my mind. I'm in a fight for control—Spirit against the flesh.

At times, all I want to do is rest, catch my breath, and wonder if I've made any progress at all in thirty-seven years. And my enemy is quite skilled and poised to scream into my head the lie that I haven't made any progress. He does it every day.

Ten years ago, I was *much* better—in my own mind. On good days, if you asked me, I was pretty much *nailing* the Christian life. I wouldn't have verbalized it this way—my behavior modification techniques would have prevented me from sounding so arrogant and presumptuous. It was more of a subconscious, internal thing. I was confident that God was applauding my performance and sharing "rave reviews" with the *Angelic Daily News.*

In reality, He was just being longsuffering with my self-trip and performance-based struggle. I was just like Peter before the crucifixion. Jesus was just tolerating my ego, blessing me in spite of myself, and overlooking a ton of self-assurance.

He was putting up with my ignorance, knowing that the longer I walked with Him, the more evident my brokenness would be, and the more massive His grace would be. He was like a knowing parent carrying on a ridiculous argument with a five-year-old. Because of the cross, He was exceedingly patient with my propensity to sin, and He loved me with unconditional grace as a result.

He Loves Us in Spite of Us

Yes, you and I are worse than we think, but God's love is greater than we think. I would never tell you consciously that I was laboring to earn God's love. I know better. That is theologically incorrect.

But many times, I was doing just that in practice. In reality, my efforts were "my working to earn something from Him." My labor for Jesus was too often self and flesh attempting to *deserve* what He had done. It was subtle and subconscious, but it was real. I was a hostage to performing for Him and attempting to gain His approval.

Worse, much of the time I was convinced that I was *succeeding!* I was good at being good, until I realized how really "not good" I was… am. Mind you, this was long after coming to Jesus in faith for salvation. I was engaged in performance-based acceptance and personal behavior modification. I was serving Him every day. I was working hard at being good…and succeeding, by my own standard of measurement.

I calculated my goodness rather generously. I was getting "a lot done for Jesus." And it was fun to serve Him. So I figured He smiled on all of my accomplishments for Him. I was proud to be exhausted for Him. I was counting the number of people "I brought to Jesus"—blah, blah, blah. I was measuring myself by comparing myself. I was winning my own game, and sure that God was playing along.

Yet there were moments when I also knew I was failing miserably. The pendulum swung widely. There were times when my heart would fail, my strength wane, and I felt like a total failure and disappointment to God. In those times, it seemed I could never do enough ministry, share Jesus with enough people, give enough money, make enough sacrifices— *ad infinitum!* On those days, my efforts and my tiny scales seemed to add up to nothing, which was terribly disheartening.

What I missed—what I have only now begun to see through a glass darkly—is that He loved me *before* all that, He loved me *through* it all (though my good works were often my idols stealing my affection from Him), and He loves me *with or without* it all. He loved me equally through all the winning, losing, and trying. He loved me patiently through all of my silly games and self-centered growth projects. He loved me even when I loved my self-improvement more than Him.

He loves me unconditionally and infinitely and perfectly, with incalculable measure!

It all has nothing to do with me. *Me* plus *all-of-me* plus *all-of-my-work* plus *all-of-my-effort* plus *all-of-my-sleepless-nights* plus *all-of-my-workaholism* plus *all-of-my-achievement* all adds up to *nothing*!

He loves me *in spite* of me. Yes, I serve Him, but not to gain His love or approval. Yes, I honor Him, but not to earn or be deserving of Him. Yes, I desire to accomplish His will and glorify Him, but not in myself and not to impress Him or others. I could never deserve Him and I have nothing to offer Him but a broken life that, apart from Him, makes nothing but messes.

I could never do or behave in any way that would make Jesus love me any more than He already does. I could never offer Him anything that He doesn't already have.

I have *all* of His capacity to love—it's *all* mine, it's *all* yours, already.

This is critical: Nothing motivates, stirs, and compels me more to worship and serve my Saviour than the fact that He loves me in spite of me.

> For the love of Christ constraineth us; because we thus judge, that if one died for all, then were all dead.—2 CORINTHIANS 5:14

Jesus in Me—My Only Hope for Goodness

Even my best self-works are like filthy rags. In my flesh is no good thing. Cancer produces only cancer. Cancer cells don't birth healthy cells. Cancer just keeps killing. My own goodness is worthless apart from Jesus.

Now before you think that's demotivating; before you think that's what causes Christians to live sinfully or casually, think again. The opposite is true! If you think you can motivate yourself to do right, just wait until you let *grace* motivate you!

Grace doesn't motivate you to sin or to abuse grace—unless you don't understand grace.

Grace—God's unconditional acceptance and love—is the only environment in which true spiritual transformation can unfold. Grace is the single greatest motivator for genuine love-based obedience and faith in action. Grace is the only climate in which God's work can unfold, and in which the Spirit of God can produce real fruit to His glory. Anything less than grace working through you is artificial fruit to self glory.

Good works don't flow out of self—ever. Goodness isn't a product of a reformed you. Salvation isn't your turning over a new leaf.

No, my tree is rotten all the way to the core. The trunk, the roots, the whole system is corrupt. For anything good to come from my existence, I must be reseeded, re-sprouted, regrown, and re-nourished from a new source altogether—grafted from scratch into a new vine with a new life source.

> *I am the vine, ye are the branches: He that abideth in me, and I in him,*
> *the same bringeth forth much fruit: for without me ye can do nothing.*
> —JOHN 15:5

Reducing Grace to Less than Amazing

Somehow we see our "new selves" after salvation as capable of accomplishing measured goodness on our own. We launch out independently to achieve and reform ourselves for God—like we owe it to Him. We take salvation and try to leverage it in our own power.

And when we visibly, measurably succeed at behavior modification, we proclaim a work of grace.

"Look at me! I'm so much better! I have really changed!" It sounds good, and it is, until we fail again. Then what happened to the 'work of grace of which we boasted? What about the struggles you've never conquered? What about the struggles you've fought over and over—what about grace then? Is it insufficient? Are you really saved? Is something broken? No—your repeat struggles and God's repeat forgiveness are what really make grace so massive and amazing!

Do you see how *self* can trump *grace* in our minds? We often mask self-effort with grace-talk, and what we really mean is, "See what I did? See what I accomplished? I could have never done it without God's grace!"

The implication is, "I was *close*. I was *almost there*. I did *most* of the work. It was mostly me. I'm really pretty good and pretty close to the goal. God's grace was what gave me that final edge, that little needed boost of confidence and power! God's grace was that small, sufficient final straw. Me, me, me—almost all me, plus that last little dose of grace, and *wow*, look at the results! Thank God for His grace!"

This seems to work on the good days. But it royally breaks down on the failing days.

In this thinking, my sin isn't really that bad and grace isn't really that great or amazing. Sin is a small hurdle that I could almost conquer alone. Jesus is a small Saviour who did a little "cross thing" to provide that edge that I needed. And my faith is my brilliant decision to tap into that God-factor that pushed me over the last little hurdle of sin. Now look at me and all that *God and I* accomplished!

"Thank you, Jesus, for Your grace! If it weren't for You, I wouldn't have made it over that last hump. If it weren't for grace I'd only be 'almost good enough.' If it weren't for You, I would have only accomplished *some* good—but thanks to You, I can accomplish *much* good. I was just 'almost great' now You've made me 'even greater!'"

The implication is that Jesus made up the slight difference I needed. This isn't a Saviour. This is a steroid. Jesus didn't rescue me; He merely enhanced my already impressive performance.

Do you see it? Sure you do. You've thought it. Just like I have. We wouldn't verbalize it this way, but that's what subtly goes on inside of us. In our minds, we're 99 percent there, and grace is that extra 1 percent steroid-boost we really needed to be *everything* God wants us to be. Whew! Thanks for God's *amazing grace!* (Like grace is a five-hour energy drink for the soul!)

Gag!

That grace isn't amazing. It's barely necessary. It's small. It's insufficient. It's just a "tipping point" of my own greatness. That grace is just a little trigger that released my amazing self! And in this thinking, I'm just on a crash course of discovering how broken I really am.

If you don't get anything else from this chapter, please get this: we are nothing. We have nothing good to offer. Jesus is everything, and grace is *His everything* given *freely* to *nothing*—namely me.

From beginning to end, salvation, growth, transformation, sanctification, service, sacrifice—from start to finish—your journey with Jesus is ALL Him, ALL grace, and ALL undeserved. Be impressed with Him. Period.

A Dead Flesh Walking in Living Grace

We like to measure greatness or progress—in others, and sadly, in ourselves. But let's be real.

Great by what measure? Great by whose standard? Great by whose box, whose list, what measuring stick? Attributing spiritual greatness is difficult in contrast to the reality of sin, grace, and Jesus. In truth, sin is exceedingly destructive, men are exceedingly sinful, and Jesus is the only good, great, awesome, amazing part of anything we believe!

Jesus is great, and His grace is great.

Most men will proclaim every one his own goodness: but a faithful man who can find?—PROVERBS 20:6

Great is the LORD, and greatly to be praised; and his greatness is unsearchable.—PSALM 145:3

Who am I? Who are you?

Paul said, "...*we are His workmanship, created in Christ Jesus unto good works...*" (Ephesians 2:10).

Jesus said, "...*without me ye can do nothing*" (John 15:5).

These statements are literal and profound. They are categorical. They flatten us. They reduce us to a zero sum factor in the whole equation. It's all Him, not me.

I'm just a sinful being with no hope. Any goodness that flows is not "my doing it for Him." Nope. Not even 1 percent! Any goodness is grace at work in me—Him, His Spirit and presence producing fruit from His hands for His glory.

I'm a sack of dying flesh with a living Saviour inside. But He loves me, in spite of me, and He chooses to work in me and through me in ways I will never comprehend or understand. I'm a glove and He's the hand. The glove doesn't boast about the beautiful painting it painted or the wonderful deeds it did. Without a hand, a glove is dead, useless, lifeless.

Saved by Grace, but Still Struggling

Sin struggles are with you for the duration. Don't get used to it, but accept it and expect it.

There isn't a coming day when you can stand in your local church and give a testimony that God has finally delivered you from pride. You won't ever wake up in this life and discover that you are no longer selfish, lustful, greedy, arrogant, or narcissistic. You have fear in ways you never understood fear. You are anxious right now about things you haven't consciously considered. You are fighting your flesh in this moment on multiple levels. And if you think you've fully and finally overcome any one of these things, you're lying to yourself.

Even if you've been saved a very long time, the flesh is still alive and well, and your transformation by God's grace is still very far from completion.

You may have created a "good-box" and conformed yourself into it. You may have modified your behavior so that everyone around you is impressed. You may have cleverly covered your bad points and managed to mask your weak places. You might have perfected a public persona that defines you as a good Christian by your measurement (or other's).

But in your heart, in the mirror, and in your conscience, you know that there are things about you that are still very broken. You know the internal struggles—the pride, the anger, the resentment, the envy, the fear, the anxiety, the doubt, the rebellion.

And so does God.

Yet He loves you. He accepts you. He smiles upon you with delight. Not because of all the good things you checked off your "good list" last week, and not because you have overcome so much bad stuff already.

Jesus and His work on the cross make you righteous in His eyes. Jesus' righteousness has been miraculously wrapped around you like a much undeserved "new wardrobe"! God sees you in Him, and that's the only thing good about you or me.

Paul said he wrestled with sin every day, and so will you. He stated it this way in Philippians:

> *Being confident of this very thing, that he which hath begun a good work*
> *in you will perform it until the day of Jesus Christ:*—PHILIPPIANS 1:6

This verse is amazing! It's a God-inspired, positive, hopeful spin on the fact that you are a mess being de-messified—from now until you see Jesus! You are unfinished. Incomplete. Awkward. Struggling.

You're not where you *were*, but not where you *will be*, and definitely not where you *want* to be!

You are damaged goods. You are a newborn, spiritual being locked in an old, sin-laden flesh, trapped between the law of sin warring in your members and the law of the Spirit of life in Christ Jesus. You are under construction, being worked on by the gracious Spirit of Almighty God—for the rest of your earthly days. This is the new you locked in an old container.

Welcome to real Christianity. Welcome to a real relationship where Jesus knows you intimately, accepts you unconditionally, walks with you personally, and works on you unceasingly. Because of Calvary, Jesus is a good forgiver! *Undeserving* meets *unconditional*. *Unable* meets *all sufficient*.

Sin struggles are here to stay, until you see Jesus. Don't *give in* to it… but yes, *accept it*. You are saved to struggle, at least for now. And to think otherwise is to believe a lie, no matter how well-meaning, how dogmatic, or how passionate—anyone telling you that you won't struggle from here to eternity isn't telling you the truth.

You are locked in a struggle, but you are not *condemned* in that struggle. We can even bring glory to God through the struggle—if we grasp what's really going on. (More on that to come!)

It's a paradox which we will more fully explore. You are saved to struggle, but not alone, not hopeless, not condemned, not judged, not guilted or shamed. You are saved by grace and you walk in grace—all day, every day—unconditional, inexhaustible, immeasurable grace. And that grace is the only resource that can produce any good, and the only reason you can get back up every single time you fail—to the magnitude of infinity times infinity.

The Only Response Is Worship

To declare, I say, at this time his righteousness: that he might be just, and the justifier of him which believeth in Jesus. Where is boasting then? It is excluded. By what law? of works? Nay: but by the law of faith.
—Romans 3:26–27

And you hath he quickened, who were dead in trespasses and sins;
—Ephesians 2:1

We tend to think with a reductionist perspective about sin and about grace. We tend to make ourselves better, Jesus smaller, and grace less amazing. That's what flesh does. Spiritual humility does the opposite.

The bottom line is, Jesus justified you, not so you could someday boast of how good you have become. The longer you're saved, the less "good" you will feel; the more aware of how utterly "ungood" you really are.

In contrast, Jesus and His sacrifice—His just grace and goodness—becomes exponentially larger on a cosmic scale. Like Paul, you will identify with the phrase, "Where is boasting?" What do I have to boast of?

My sin? My brokenness? My pathetic attempts to modify bad behavior? It's laughable!

I was a wreck. I still am. But I believed in Jesus. In all my sin, with all my faults, messes, and misery—I believed.

He justified. He responded to the law of faith, and placed my sin on His cross. He quickened me. He brought me back to life. And since that moment, He is my life—in every way the statement can possibly be interpreted or explained—yes, He is my life.

Sin is cancer on a massive, cosmic, nuclear scale! Jesus is a Saviour on an even greater scale! You and I are but sinful beings that He chose to love and save.

Before salvation, my clearer understanding of sin pushes me to my knees before Jesus, asking for mercy. After salvation, my growing awareness of sin pushes me downward in dependence upon Jesus. The sin struggle in me keeps me humbly aware of who I really am and fully resting in His grace and not my own attempt at behavior modification.

My desperate condition *before* salvation leaves me with only one option—*fall on my face and thank God for mercy.*

My desperate condition *after* salvation leaves me with only one option—*fall on my face, worship Him for His undeserved love and grace!*

> *And when I saw him, I fell at his feet as dead. And he laid his right hand upon me, saying unto me, Fear not; I am the first and the last:*
> —REVELATION 1:17

PART THREE

Real Renewal

Seven

Newborn

What It Really Means to Be "Born in Jesus"

Dana and I are blessed to have three children. On three unforgettable, pinnacle days of our marriage journey, God miraculously invaded our home with new life and new birth. And for the last twenty-three years, we have enjoyed real relationships with these three wonderful individuals whom God allows us to call our family!

I must confess, my children came into the world with some serious issues—which isn't surprising if you know me. They couldn't walk, talk, eat, or sustain themselves in any way. I know that's shocking, but it's true.

And things got *worse* before they got *better!* They made a lot of messes as they grew. They tried to destroy themselves every day in a variety of creative ways. At times, they acted like monkeys—especially my boys. They were like little suicidal primates—hurting themselves, breaking stuff, fighting with each other, and generally wreaking havoc.

While there was no doubt about their humanity, their behavior often left us and others wondering. Suffice it to say, they were human, but they were very *dysfunctional* humans. They weren't *becoming* human—they were 100 percent human. No doubt—these were man-children. But they really had no grasp of life-giving, life-sustaining human behavior.

They were human but not *mature* humans.

This was shocking and disappointing to say the least. When we signed on to be parents of other humans, we had higher expectations. So, when we received *immature* humans, we took them back and tried to exchange them for more intelligent models. None were available, and that's when we were informed that parenting is a commitment to unconditional acceptance of early-stage human beings, and long-term nurturing toward functional maturity.

In other words, parenting was going to be long, messy, sleepless, costly *hard work!* On the flip side of that coin however, parenting is a delightful, loving, wonderful relationship that massively overshadows all of the potential negatives. Aside from the monkey-messes, parenting is amazing!

Individualism and Behaviorism

Jesus told Nicodemus: *"Marvel not that I said unto thee, Ye must be born again"* (John 3:7).

Peter wrote to new believers that they were, *"...born again, not of corruptible seed, but of incorruptible, by the word of God, which liveth and abideth for ever"* (1 Peter 1:23).

This is great news, but what exactly does it mean?

Go with me a moment. We all tend to associate our *identity* (or individuality) with our *behavior*. We define ourselves by what we do. Our first question to new acquaintances is "What do you do?" Our answers vary, "I'm a carpenter, a plumber, an attorney, a teacher, a nurse...."

We define ourselves by our pursuits, accomplishments, abilities, and vocations. This is the norm of American individualism.

Thus, when we enter into real Christianity, we are tempted to define ourselves by "what we do." This puts us on the ladder of works to begin the climb toward God. From early in our journey this places us into a wrong mindset. Rather than walking *with* Him, we are performing *for* Him. We are tempted to define our Christian identity by *behavior* rather than *birth*. We are tempted to think that our acceptance is a product of our accomplishments.

In Bible times, a person's identity was more a function of family heritage than it is today. That's why you'll often read a Bible name followed by, "...the son of...." Prior to American individualism and the breakdown of the biblical family, people defined themselves by their families—by birth, not behavior.

This is vital. God defines you by your *birth*, not your *behavior*. You belong to Him because of your *belief*.

Christianity becomes incredibly complex and unfulfilling when we define our identity by our behavior. In other words, "I'm a good Christian because I (fill in the blank with a list of things good Christians do)." Or, "I'm not a good Christian because I (fill in the blank with something you did wrong recently)."

This is always a game. There's always something good for which I can proverbially "pat myself on the back," and there's always something sinful for which I can "beat myself up." Behavior-based identity is a trap that hinges on my mood swings or my environment. I'm my own arbiter. Whether I'm "in or out of the club" at any given moment is determined, not by God's unwavering love or grace, but by my perception of my own performance for Him—self-evaluation (which is always inaccurate).

In real Christianity, identity is determined solely by birth. Jesus accepts you because you are *born* in Him, not because you *behave* for Him. This is an incredibly liberating and wonderful realization. I've known Christians who were saved for many years before they ever understood this. Though they were saved by grace, they were working hard to achieve some level of "Christian" behavior about which they could "feel better" and feel "in God's good graces." They live like orphans at an orphanage, trying to appease an angry headmaster.

As a side note, please don't jump to the conclusion that I'm saying "any behavior" is acceptable to God. That's not the case. We'll get to that. It's just that my behavior doesn't determine His love for me.

Behaviorism leads us to one of two tragic and extreme positions. When I'm looking through the lens of my failures, it becomes horribly oppressive and discouraging. When I'm looking through the lens of my perceived successes (through self-evaluation) it becomes incredibly arrogant and presumptuous. Simply put, in behaviorism I'm either doing *poorly*, in which case I guilt and shame myself, or I'm doing *well*, in which case I congratulate myself into thinking I'm on God's favorites list. Both positions are prideful and take me off course in my walk with Jesus.

Newborn in Jesus

When God explains your new relationship with Him, He uses the metaphor of a new baby being born to loving parents. What a beautiful picture! In the next few pages we're going to break it down into four simple principles:

- You are born as a 100% new creature.

- You are born into 100% acceptance.
- You are born with 100% security.
- You are born into 100% new potential.

The big takeaway of this chapter is that *Jesus accepts you by birth— not behavior.*

It's just like me with my own children. I accepted them into my family by their birth. They did nothing to deserve my love, they do nothing to earn it or keep it—they have it freely and unconditionally for the rest of their lives, simply because they are mine. I'm their father. Though I'm sinful and imperfect, I still love my own without reservation or condition.

Am I interested in their behavior? Of course. Does their behavior determine their belonging or identity or acceptance? Not even a little bit. Their relationship to me is in *no way* dependent upon their behavior. It's all about their birth.

Let's dive in…

Newborn = 100% New Creature

New babies are wonderful, but they are a mess! And they are professional mess-makers! Wow, was parenting a wake-up call to me and my wife. I'll spare you the details, but these new babies were just gross—in a cute way, of course. For all the cooing, cuddling, and wooing that family and friends poured over them—there was another side entirely! Behind closed doors, under the baby-fresh smell, and feather-soft skin—believe me—it wasn't pretty.

In all seriousness, was I surprised? Not really. Actually, we did our best to be equipped! We understood that these creatures were new humans, and would require a lot of learning, growing, and struggling.

So when you were born in Christ, you were made a new creature. This is really big! Look at it.

Therefore if any man be in Christ, he is a new creature: old things are passed away; behold, all things are become new.—2 CORINTHIANS 5:17

For in Christ Jesus neither circumcision availeth any thing, nor uncircumcision, but a new creature.—GALATIANS 6:15

Whereby are given unto us exceeding great and precious promises: that by these ye might be partakers of the divine nature, having escaped the corruption that is in the world through lust.—2 PETER 1:4

These verses teach me that my salvation was monumental. It was a complete spiritual rebuild. Being a new creature, or being a partaker of the divine nature, is no small reforming of something old or sinful. This isn't a fresh paint job. It literally means that God crucified your sin nature—the core of your spiritual being called the "old man"—and created within you a new nature.

Knowing this, that our old man is crucified with him, that the body of sin might be destroyed, that henceforth we should not serve sin.
—ROMANS 6:6

This is bigger than you think. It's not God sharing space with your old nature. You're not a spiritual schizophrenic with dueling natures. You are a new creature 100 percent. This is internal, it's spiritual, and it's absolutely true.

You do have an internal struggle—what the Apostle Paul called "the power of sin in me." But that's not the same as your sin nature that was crucified with Christ. (We'll examine the power of sin later in Chapter 9. So hang in there.)

When you trusted Christ as Saviour, God didn't move in next to your sinful nature. He crucified your sinful nature on the cross and recreated you as a new creature, spiritually.

This doesn't mean you don't still sin or have the capacity to do wrong. It means, for the first time in your life, you are alive spiritually and now have a nature that can mature in relationship with Jesus. It means, for the first time, you are not under the control of a sinful nature that you inherited from Adam.

You were a baby at birth, but you were 100 percent human. You weren't *becoming* human. You were all human, but very immature and needing growth. So it is with your salvation. You are not becoming a new creature—you are 100 percent new creature, even though it will take the rest of your life for that new creature to mature and unlearn all the things that your old sin nature taught your flesh.

This is a critical realization for this reason: If you believe it is your *nature* to sin, you will never believe you can mature and enjoy victory over sin. If you still have a sin nature, then sin is just *natural* and there's nothing you can do about it. But if the Bible is true and you are a new creature, then you have all the potential of realizing and experiencing that new nature in a million ways in the years ahead and for all of eternity.

Therefore if any man be in Christ, he is a new creature: old things are passed away; behold, all things are become new.—2 CORINTHIANS 5:17

In other words, when Christ saved you, He wasn't just remodeling the old you. He was crucifying the old you and a new you was born in Him. This is the spiritual reality, but it's hard to accept, because our new nature is born into a body of flesh with a mind that's well trained to sin. For the rest of your life, your flesh (your mind and physical desires) will war against your new nature—fighting for control. This will make you feel like your old sin nature is still alive and well. But that's a lie.

Accepting the idea that I'm a new creature is a faith thing before it's a feeling. It doesn't feel true! It feels like I'm still a proficient sinner with a belief in Jesus. I *am* a proficient sinner, but salvation kills the "genetic source" of that sin and births a new nature within—the Divine nature. In other words, spiritually, I have God's genetics—God's Spirit—firmly woven into the very source of my being at the very moment of salvation.

When your new nature came alive, your old nature died. How do you know this? Primarily because God said it clearly in Romans 6:6. But another indicator is your new desires. Paul touched on this in Romans 7.

> For I know that in me (that is, in my flesh,) dwelleth no good thing: for to will is present with me; but how to perform that which is good I find not. For the good that I would I do not: but the evil which I would not, that I do.—ROMANS 7:18–19

Do you see the reference to his *will*—his new desires? That *will* is evidence of a new nature—a new Spirit deep within driving new intentions and new desires. The struggle of the Christian life is in allowing that new nature to have its way, while the flesh fights for its old sin habits. We'll come back to this thought.

For now, it's vital that you accept the truth of Scripture—in Christ, you are spiritually a new creature. Your nature is no longer a sin nature. Your root identity and reality is that you are *in Christ*. You are fully in Him—sort of like a new baby being fully human, but needing twenty years of education and maturity.

Your new desires are evidence of the fact that God's Spirit came into you and re-birthed you as a new creature. This also means, when you sin, you are acting *contrary* to who you really are. You are not merely a sinner saved. You are a saint that still sins. The two are very different. Let me illustrate.

My friend Derrick has a son, Titus, who is three years old. Titus loves to play like he's a puppy. For the record—he isn't. He's as human as I am. But Titus really puts on a good puppy act. He barks, whimpers, crawls around on all fours, and even drinks water from a bowl. But none of that makes him a real puppy. He's just a boy acting like a puppy. His nature is not puppy.

So, after salvation, your new nature is godly, inhabited by God's Holy Spirit. But your flesh and mind are well trained in behaving like a sinner. The fact that you can still sin doesn't mean you don't have a new nature. It simply means that you are not behaving consistently with who you really are—yet. You haven't matured.

Sometimes it's really hard for me to believe that there's anything good or godly within me. But in spite of my flesh, there is, by God's grace. This is God's promise. Underneath my flesh, there's a new set of desires—the *will* to be like Jesus. A sin nature doesn't produce that.

Newborn = 100% Accepted

To the praise of the glory of his grace, wherein he hath made us accepted in the beloved.—EPHESIANS 1:6

On a scale of 1–10, if 10 means God fully accepts you, and 1 means you're in big trouble, where do you rate?

Let me ask it another way, "Where do you *deserve* to be rated? Or where do you *feel* like you rate?"

How about this—where did my children rate with me the moment they were born? As my newborns they rated 10+! They were absolutely, fully accepted just as they were—even with all of their messes.

So, where do you rate with God? Because of Jesus, you rate 10+, and you always will. It's not a sliding scale that vacillates. God isn't emotionally unstable or up and down when it comes to His love for you. He is steadfast and unchanging. You always rate 10+, not because of yourself, but because of Jesus. You are 100 percent accepted and always will be.

There are two contexts of the word "acceptance" in Scripture when it comes to Christians. The first is in relationship to Jesus and our belonging to Him. That's where we are told in Ephesians 1:6 that we are accepted in the beloved: *"To the praise of the glory of his grace, wherein he hath made us accepted in the beloved."*

The second is in the context of our labor—our faith in action—being acceptable to Him. *"Wherefore we labour, that, whether present or absent, we may be accepted of him"* (2 Corinthians 5:9). The point here is that we can spiritually labor for the wrong reasons, in the wrong ways, with sinful agendas or motives. This verse is referring to pure-hearted, faith-filled service, which is meaningful and well pleasing to Jesus.

It's referring to our ministering being honorable to Him, but it does not imply that our relationship with Him could ever be called into question. Think of it this way—my children are 100 percent accepted by me as they are, but their behavior isn't always acceptable to me.

We will examine God's heart for your behavior later, but for now you must delight in this fact. You could never be *more accepted* by God. Anything you ever do to serve or honor Him is *never* to earn or deserve His acceptance. Why is this realization important?

Think about how hard it would be for my kids to know, love, and enjoy me if they were always worried about my "kicking them out of the family." If my acceptance of them were *conditional*, they would live with great fear and anxiety, which would cripple our relationship. They would find it very difficult, or even impossible, to be close to me personally. Like orphans, they would relate to me as headmaster rather than as sons relating to a father.

If you believe God is "on/off" with you based upon your behavior, you will always see Him as *Sheriff* and never as *Saviour*. You will see Him and relate to Him as Führer rather than as Father. He doesn't want a cop and criminal relationship. All of His work on the cross paved the way for His grace to extend to you a Father-child relationship.

Accept it. You are accepted.

I can hear you arguing this point in your mind. "Yeah, but what about what I did yesterday? What about the ways I'm struggling right now? What about my faults?"

Sure, you have some growing to do. God isn't surprised by your sin. In fact, He became sin for you—that is to say, He became your sin to save you from it! God's work in you isn't complete—not by a long shot. But you are still absolutely accepted, and you don't have to wrestle one more minute with guilt or shame from your past or present, because in Jesus Christ, you are a new creature. You are God's newborn child, and He fully loves you, even with all of your sin.

The thing about babies and children—they don't really ever stop making messes. The messes just look different over time. In fact, some argument could be made that our adult messes are a lot messier than our infant messes were! Even as we mature, we're still sort of messy aren't we?

That's why acceptance and grace are so critical to your understanding. You're messy. You always will be—to some degree—until you see Jesus. Your messes will change. Hopefully you'll grow. Hopefully you will win a lot of battles by God's grace. But a mess-less life and a mess-less Christianity doesn't exist this side of Heaven.

Understanding that God welcomes you into a relationship—mess and all—is vital to being able to relax, enjoy, and know Him. He doesn't call you to anxiety and a spirit of fearfulness. He calls you to trust in Him with a spirit of restfulness.

Do you know why God can love you fully in spite of your messes? Because of Jesus on the cross and the massive sacrificial and substitutionary work He did there. The cross is *that big!* It overwhelms all of your messiness in the eyes of God.

In this, God can still be *just* in dealing with your sin on the cross; but also be *justifier* in forgiving and embracing you, to make you a new creature. Usually the just and the justifier are two different parties. Think of a legal system. The judge (or society) demands justice—payment for a crime, while the defense attorney plays justifier, working to mediate the payment for the crime in some reasonable way.

God is both! He is the *Just Judge* who rightfully demands payment for sin. But He is also the defense attorney—*Justifier*—providing full payment for that sin and justifying the sinner.

> *To declare, I say, at this time his righteousness: that he might be just, and the justifier of him which believeth in Jesus.*—ROMANS 3:26

You are not accepted by God on the basis of your behavior—ever, in any sense. You are accepted on the basis of Jesus and grace. You are accepted because you belong to Him by birth.

Do you feel that you have to somehow fight, serve, or labor to gain God's acceptance? Not true! You could never be more accepted than you are simply by birth.

Newborn = 100% Secure

> *In whom ye also trusted, after that ye heard the word of truth, the gospel of your salvation: in whom also after that ye believed, ye were sealed with that holy Spirit of promise,*—EPHESIANS 1:13

And grieve not the holy Spirit of God, whereby ye are sealed unto the day of redemption.—EPHESIANS 4:30

This is called *eternal security*, and it's really cool! Nothing can cause you to lose your new nature. It is permanent. Salvation is birth—and birth is irreversible. You cannot lose your acceptance with God. You cannot do anything to ever become "unborn" in God's family.

You *can* live against or inconsistently with your nature. You *can* stay carnal and immature. You *can* behave poorly and inconsistently as a Christian. But you *cannot* ever become lost again! Spiritual birth is everlasting.

Think of it on a genetic level. Your physical identity is connected to your parents by genetic code. Every cell of your body contains the genetic architecture of your physical being that connects you to every member of your bloodline. It's unchangeable and verifiable. No matter what you do to disassociate from your family, you could never rewrite the permanent genetic code etched at the microscopic level.

Good news! When you were born as a new creature, it was a genetic thing, spiritually speaking. Look at what God says:

Not by works of righteousness which we have done, but according to his mercy he saved us, by the washing of regeneration, and renewing of the Holy Ghost;—TITUS 3:5

The word *regeneration* is like saying, "You've been re-gened!" You have God's nature in you now. If your spiritual being had "cells"—you have God's genes written into every cell. And God calls this your *seal* or your *earnest*—which is like saying "the downpayment." God's Spirit in you—indwelling your new nature—is His identity etched into your spiritual being permanently and irrevocably.

> *In whom ye also trusted, after that ye heard the word of truth, the gospel of your salvation: in whom also after that ye believed, ye were sealed with that holy Spirit of promise, Which is the earnest of our inheritance until the redemption of the purchased possession, unto the praise of his glory.*—EPHESIANS 1:13–14

> *If we believe not, yet he abideth faithful: he cannot deny himself.* —2 TIMOTHY 2:13

Etch it in your heart. As a new creature, you are born into absolute security. Nothing can remove the seal of God's Spirit. Nothing can rewrite your spiritual genetics. Nothing can ever threaten or change your security with Jesus. Behavior didn't bring you to Jesus. Behavior can't remove you from Him.

He accepts you by birth.

Newborn = 100% New Potential

Finally, being a newborn in Jesus means you have unbelievable potential for growth and personal transformation. This begins with internal transformation, but it always works its way outward in external behavior. As you grow in godly character you will also grow in godly behavior. Look at Peter's instruction to believers:

> *Grace and peace be multiplied unto you through the knowledge of God, and of Jesus our Lord, According as his divine power hath given unto us all things that pertain unto life and godliness, through the knowledge of him that hath called us to glory and virtue: Whereby are given unto us exceeding great and precious promises: that by these ye might be partakers of the divine nature, having escaped the corruption that is in the world through lust. And beside this, giving all diligence, add to your faith virtue; and to virtue knowledge; And to knowledge temperance; and to temperance patience; and to patience godliness; And to godliness*

*brotherly kindness; and to brotherly kindness charity. For if these things
be in you, and abound, they make you that ye shall neither be barren
nor unfruitful in the knowledge of our Lord Jesus Christ. But he that
lacketh these things is blind, and cannot see afar off, and hath forgotten
that he was purged from his old sins.*—2 PETER 1:2–9

*As newborn babes, desire the sincere milk of the word, that ye may grow
thereby:*—1 PETER 2:2

*But grow in grace, and in the knowledge of our Lord and Saviour
Jesus Christ. To him be glory both now and for ever. Amen.*
—2 PETER 3:18

My children, as 100 percent humans, were born with amazing
potential to grow, learn, and mature. As of this writing, they are entering
adulthood, starting their own families, and pursuing God's will for their
future. Wow, have they grown! They not only talk and walk and feed
themselves, they are moving forward in marvelous ways. They amaze and
delight me with their abilities, gifts, and personalities. Watching them
grow has been the delight of my life!

As a newborn creature in Christ, you too have amazing potential
to grow and mature. You are a partaker of the Divine nature—which is
a colossal statement! Expressing that nature and growing into the image
of Jesus is now the journey of the rest of your life. Progress will be slow
and at times painful, but never forget this—you have all the very real
potential of maturity. It's already in you.

It's no surprise to God that you aren't mature. Your messes are why
you need Him and His grace. You'll never be as mature as you want to
be—practically speaking. For the rest of your earthly journey, you are
a growing Christian. You will always wish you were somewhere further
along. That's the nature of the growth process.

My kids have rarely ever just really enjoyed being the age they were. They always wanted to be the next age, the next grade, the next place in life. In first grade they wanted to be big third graders. In junior high they wanted to be senior highers. In senior high they wanted to be seniors. In twelfth grade they wanted to be in college. In college they wanted to be married. And the story goes on.

If you're not careful, you will focus so much on "how far you have to go" that you will forget to enjoy Jesus on the journey today! You'll forget that you aren't where you were, and you aren't where you will be!

As a newborn with great potential, you are embarking on a growth journey that will be tediously tiring and painfully slow. You will want to grow *faster*. You will be tempted to berate yourself for not being better. One of the great secrets of enjoying the journey is learning to be very thankful for where you are right now with Jesus.

It's a faith thing. Knowing He's at work and growing you in His grace brings you to a point of patient confidence—optimistically waiting in faith for His work to continue, even when you really want Him to hurry up.

> *Being confident of this very thing, that he which hath begun a good work in you will perform it until the day of Jesus Christ:*—PHILIPPIANS 1:6

> *But let patience have her perfect work, that ye may be perfect and entire, wanting nothing.*—JAMES 1:4

Embrace Your New Nature, by Faith

Many Christians wrestle with accepting the idea of a new nature and all that comes with it. I hope you will get over this hurdle quickly and never look back. You aren't the same person you were before your salvation.

Physically you are. Emotionally and intellectually you are. But spiritually you are completely new.

What if a caterpillar refused to believe its potential to be a butterfly? What if a butterfly refused to accept that it was anything other than a spray-painted, remodeled worm? Forget flying. Forget enjoying new life after metamorphosis. Forget any thinking beyond "worm-brain." You'll just forget growing altogether. You'll sit down in the mire of your flesh and say, "Well, this is just who I am. I'll never be any different."

The fact is, a butterfly's only hope of flying is to first *accept* its new identity—to *believe* it. Likewise, you will never move beyond your belief. Faith is the foundation of all spiritual growth and maturity. Faith is the language of your relationship with Jesus! He responds to faith. He is pleased by faith. He transforms you as a product of your faith.

If you don't *believe* you are a new creature and accept it by faith, you'll never enjoy it in this life. Maturity begins with faith—belief. Jesus cannot do His work in you if you believe you're merely a remodeled sinner. You'll always believe you're "faking it." The truth is that when you *sin,* you're faking it—because that's against your nature. When you are walking in faith and love with Jesus, you're *never* faking it. That's the most consistent thing you can do in your new nature in Jesus. That's who you *really are*, whether you feel like it or not.

The first step to really enjoying Jesus, and who you are in Him, is to believe it. Accept your new identity. It's a fact of grace.

For I delight in the law of God after the inward man:—Romans 7:22

But now in Christ Jesus ye who sometimes were far off are made nigh by the blood of Christ.—Ephesians 2:13

Eight

New Life, Old Flesh
Understanding the "in between"
Component of Salvation

I really hate snakes. They truly creep me out on every level. And don't tell me, "It's not poisonous." That is completely irrelevant. It's not about poison. It never was. It's about creepy. I just don't like things that max out my "creep-o-meter."

Not long ago, our family moved into a home with a basement. As we settled, I decided to reclaim the basement space and make it semi-useable—especially since I needed a quiet place to study. After several days with a shop-vac, some trash bags, several gallons of insect spray, and lots of sweeping, cleaning, painting, and fixing—the basement was officially clean and useable, though still unfinished.

I picked a corner, threw down a carpet remnant, and set up shop. It was sort of rough and dark—but it was quiet and private, which made it perfect for studying or writing. I began spending a lot of time in that basement corner.

One random afternoon, I bounded down the stairs and into the study only to be met by what I first thought was a lamp cord—unattached to a lamp. I paused, did a double-take, and found myself being gawked at by a snake—*in my study!* This is not good.

I froze—looking at him. He froze—looking at me. We were both thinking the same thing. *What are you doing in my space?* And I think he was thinking, *By the way, thanks for the nice carpet!*

A friend of mine happened to be upstairs helping us hang doors so I yelled, "Dana, tell Tim to come down here." With that, I grabbed a random piece of wood trim, and pinned my harmless oppressor to the carpet until help could arrive. When Tim arrived on scene, he laughed.

"Tim, I don't care what you do. Laugh, call me a coward, call me a girl, tell the whole world. None of it matters or changes anything about this. I don't do snakes."

Again he laughed and said, "Well, do you do mice?"

"Yes, I do mice," I said.

"Well, if that were a mouse, I would be on the table screaming with my daughters. I don't do mice. So, I'll do your snake if you will do my mice." With that, we had an agreement, and Tim removed the snake from my domain.

Would you believe, two days later, the snake was *back*—but that's when he boarded "the shovel express" straight to eternity. And for several days I nearly killed every black lamp cord in our home! I was twitchy to say the least! Suffice it to say, my whole family was creeped out by the basement.

For the next several days, we plugged holes, fixed cracks, and sufficiently rid the area of our unwelcome friends. But a few days later I got the brainy idea to play a prank on my wife and kids. I purchased a little black rubber snake from Walmart.

Back at home, I carefully set the plastic snake on the bottom step, set up my video camera, and calmly asked one family member at a time to "run down to the basement" and grab something for me. Such fun! One at a time, each family member freaked out, squealed, and ran back upstairs. It was awesome.

Here's the insane part of this story. After the last person was pranked, I promptly forgot about the joke. A few hours later, I bounded down the stairs only to freak out at *my own* prank! I'm talking complete panic and random bodily spasms—over my own joke.

But wait, it gets even crazier. For the next week I actually scared myself with that stupid rubber snake no less than five times! My family still doesn't know this, but God truly gave them justice. I think He was laughing harder than anyone. Every time I went into the basement, I saw the fake snake, had a momentary creep out, then moved the snake to another location—only to forget about it, until I saw it again a couple days later.

On the fifth time, I finally tossed the plastic snake into an exterior trash can where I would never see it again!

Here's the point. Inside—emotionally, spiritually, intellectually—we are more complex than we realize. We are fully capable of experiencing conflict between perception and reality. We often experience a collision between truth and emotion.

How in the world could my emotions continually go nuts over something my brain knew was fake? Why couldn't my heart accept truth that my brain clearly understood? Why couldn't I make those internal connections? Why did my emotions keep lying to me over and over again? And what does all this have to do with life in Jesus Christ?

Here's the big idea of this chapter. As a Christian—I'm not who I used to be, I'm not who I will be! Now that looks like a simple statement, but there's a lot to it. Let's explore some truth that will help you process all the moments where your emotions and actions work against truth.

This chapter will shine some more light on the "new creature" concept that we studied in the last chapter.

The Lies of Secular Thought

You are more than a body. You are more than randomly evolved biological matter being swept along by spontaneous events strung together by fate and cosmic evolutionary processes. You are not an accident, and you are not "just what you see in the mirror." There's a lot more to you than just a "sack of meat."

Secular thought is so brainless and morbid when it comes to the big questions. Self-help psychology tries hard to *avoid* truth—escapism. Why? Because secular thought doesn't have solid answers to deep questions— like "Where did I come from?" "Why am I here?" "What is the purpose of life?" and "Where am I going?" The answers that secularists provide for these questions are always hopeless.

Secularists say you are "randomly evolved biological matter." Which is to say, you have no meaningful origin, no intelligent purpose, no significance or value, and no future but nothingness. That's hopeless.

Secularists also say there is no God. Man is god, so worship the creature, not a creator. The conclusion is, you are nothing, but you are god. You are the nothing god of nothing. Congratulations! Don't you feel special?

Culture says you're just a "sack of meat," so live for immediate pleasure because nothing else matters. Take the path of least resistance and immediate gratification—if it feels good, do it; follow your heart.

This deceptive belief system breaks down with one word—*conscience*. Randomly evolved matter doesn't have a conscience. Spontaneous evolution doesn't etch eternal moral values and a sense of good and evil into its genetic code. Cosmic primordial soup doesn't give birth to life that *instinctively* worships.

In every people group, every nation, and every era of human history—from the most civilized to the least, you will find people *worshiping!* Even the atheist worships self by declaring "there is no God"—*everybody* worships. Everybody subjects themselves to a moral code that reveals the existence of their conscience, hence the existence of a moral authority (God)!

Conscience is the knowledge of right and wrong—the internal awareness of moral absolutes. It is the intrinsic nature in us all that calls us to worship.

> *Because that which may be known of God is manifest in them; for God hath shewed it unto them.*—ROMANS 1:19

Yes, you are much more than a body—let's look deeper.

A Multi-Faceted Creation

God tells us the truth about ourselves:

> *And the very God of peace sanctify you wholly; and I pray God your whole spirit and soul and body be preserved blameless unto the coming of our Lord Jesus Christ.*—1 THESSALONIANS 5:23

> *For as the body without the spirit is dead, so faith without works is dead also.*—JAMES 2:26

> *For which cause we faint not; but though our outward man perish, yet the inward man is renewed day by day.*—2 CORINTHIANS 4:16

These verses explain that you are made up of three parts in one being—spirit, soul, and body. (As a side note, it's nearly impossible to absolutely separate these three parts of your being—especially soul and spirit—as they are very intricately connected and interwoven, and the words are sometimes used interchangeably in Scripture. Please understand as you read, this is a generalization of God's very complex creative design. Yet, God's Word indicates enough distinction for us to understand His work and how it unfolds within.) Understanding real salvation begins with understanding how Jesus is working in the different facets of our being. Let's define each.

Body—This is what some call your "earth-suit" or "flesh-suit." It's a sack of meat that the rest of you wears while you live on earth. You feed it, rest it, exercise it, care for it, and nurture it. When sick, you take it to the doctor. When hurt, you mend it. When needy, you try to fulfill it. And when it dies, you exit it and continue existing apart from it.

Over time, your body ages and breaks. Paul said, in this we "groan"— wishing we could have a new body that matches our new nature!

For in this we groan, earnestly desiring to be clothed upon with our house which is from heaven: For we that are in this tabernacle do groan, being burdened: not for that we would be unclothed, but clothed upon, that mortality might be swallowed up of life.—2 CORINTHIANS 5:2, 4

Soul—This is what occupies your body—the inner you. It's your mind, will, and emotions. It's what the Bible often calls your *heart*. This is your *thinker* (or your intellect), your *chooser* (your will), and your *feeler* (your emotions).

Thinker, chooser, feeler—your soul is complex. It's the sum total of your inner man that processes and wills you forward through every experience and relationship. It's your personality and uniqueness. It's the real you inside of the "flesh-suit."

> *Keep thy heart with all diligence; for out of it are the issues of life.*
> —PROVERBS 4:23

> *Search me, O God, and know my heart: try me, and know my thoughts:*
> —PSALM 139:23

Spirit—This is the source of your deepest being. Before salvation, this was essentially your sin nature—dead to God spiritually. This was your sinful root system that was fallen and could not come to God. God calls this your "old man." Your *source*, your spiritual genetics were proficient at producing sin. Remember the cancer illustration? This part of you was the production center of the condition called "sin."

After salvation, your old man is crucified with Christ—completely dead. Remember, this is not a behavioral thing, it's a biblical thing. You may not feel like your sin nature died, but it did. Your new nature is alive to God which makes you His new creature. Your spirit is reborn and made new by your faith in Jesus. God's Holy Spirit is now within you, enabling your new nature to know God and experience His grace and transforming presence in your life.

> *Howbeit when he, the Spirit of truth, is come, he will guide you into all truth....*—JOHN 16:13

> *Now we have received, not the spirit of the world, but the spirit which is of God; that we might know the things that are freely given to us of God.*—1 CORINTHIANS 2:12

> *In whom ye also trusted, after that ye heard the word of truth, the gospel of your salvation: in whom also after that ye believed, ye were sealed with that holy Spirit of promise,*—EPHESIANS 1:13

God's work within each facet of our beings connects with my snake illustration—here's how. God desires for me to be led by His Spirit in all of life. The Holy Spirit is within me to dictate truth to my soul (mind, will, emotions). He desires to anchor my thoughts, emotions, and choices and direct them accordingly. He desires to lead me into behavior that is "like Jesus" or in line with the "mind of Christ."

Let this mind be in you, which was also in Christ Jesus:—PHILIPPIANS 2:5

As God's Spirit leads my new nature, it directs my soul which then dictates to the body how to act or behave. It's a top down approach to living that flows from God's Spirit within—God's Word calls this "walking in the Spirit" (Galatians 5:16, 25). But it's a life-long process and a daily struggle to live this way. Before salvation, it wasn't even an option. My sin nature pretty much called the shots, except in areas where family or culture had forced behavior modification (a temporary attempt to tame my sin nature).

The snake story shows how the three parts of my being can break down and mislead me.

First, my spirit knows the truth that should make me free from fear. I should be able to walk right past that rubber snake and tell my mind, will, and emotions, "It's fake, forget about it."

Second, my soul (mind, will, and emotions) should process the truth with a calm *emotional* response (no creep factor), intelligent *thought* (that's not a real snake), and reasonable *choice*.

Third, my body should obey and make it happen—"Keep walking and don't experience any physical or emotional response toward that rubber snake."

But that's not what happens. Soul grasps immediate control. Mind, will, and emotions do an emergency override of truth and spirit. It happens so quickly that I don't even realize it. Emotions start calling ridiculous plays. Here's what it looks like:

First, spirit gets shut down. Truth is irrelevant. Urgency leaps right over truth.

Second, emotions declare a "snake emergency." Mind responds with logic about snakes. Emotions respond with fear and paranoia.

Third, body responds with adrenalin release, increased heart rate, heightened nerves, and spastic reflexes.

In a fraction of a second, soul is misinformed and lying. Emotions are screaming bad information and calling for bad decisions.

In this case it's funny. We laugh at the thought of me, alone in my basement, repeatedly "spazzing out." No harm done. Truth is quickly recovered, emotions are reprimanded for lying, and soul starts to process truth and dictate different responses. Emotions settle and eventually submit to truth, and body starts obeying truth by either ignoring the snake or throwing it in the trash. Several minutes pass before body settles down, heart rate slows, and normalcy returns.

On a much larger scale, this process is far more destructive. Every day we ignore truth and follow feelings into disaster and regret. Whenever the flesh rules, it always discounts truth and seeks self-gratification. It always believes the lies of emotions, which leads to bad decisions and broken lives.

The world's value system places body and soul in control! This is "soulish" living, and it will always lead you down the wrong road with misinformation.

In Jesus, for the first time in your life, you have a new nature with the spiritual capacity to yield to a different master. You have access to absolute truth through Jesus and His Word. You can now begin to experience a total renewing of your mind and the transformation of your life—based upon truth. This is only possible because of Jesus and the new creature that He has created you to be through salvation.

Salvation Is a Multi-Faceted Miracle

Keeping the multi-facet creation (spirit, soul, body) in mind—let's look at salvation through this lens. What we're about to study is critical to understanding salvation. Much of this book has been building to this point, so take your time through this section.

What we're about to see is woven into nearly every page of the New Testament. It's an *accurate theological framework* for understanding Jesus' work in you. It can be verified by hundreds of Bible passages. Due to space constraints, we will see only a few. But if you will lock in on this framework, it will make a major light bulb come on in your head. Much of God's Word will make more sense to you.

First, lets take a look at a few passages to get a scriptural view:

But of him are ye in Christ Jesus, who of God is made unto us wisdom, and righteousness, and sanctification, and redemption:
—1 Corinthians 1:30

Key words—*righteousness, sanctification, redemption*. Remember those words—they correlate to the work of salvation in your life.

But after that the kindness and love of God our Saviour toward man appeared, Not by works of righteousness which we have done, but according to his mercy he saved us, by the washing of regeneration, and renewing of the Holy Ghost; Which he shed on us abundantly through Jesus Christ our Saviour; That being justified by his grace, we should be made heirs according to the hope of eternal life.—Titus 3:4–7

Key phrases—*washing of regeneration, renewing of the Holy Ghost,* and *heirs according to the hope of eternal life.* Hold on to those, they correlate to the same three dynamics.

What do these and many other passages teach about salvation?

Each verse shows us that the work of salvation is more than a one-time event. It's also a *three-part process.* Salvation begins with *new birth,* but that's only a first step of a larger process that unfolds throughout our earthly lives and culminates when we see Jesus face to face.

- Your spirit was made new *instantly* when you believed—this is the *new birth.*
- Your soul is being renewed *daily* by the Spirit of God—this is referred to as the *renewing of your mind.*
- Your body will be made new *eventually*—this is final *redemption.*

Think in terms of these three words—*regeneration, renewal, redemption*:

- **Regeneration**—Your spirit was *regenerated* (re-gened) the moment you trusted Jesus.

  Not by works of righteousness which we have done, but according to his mercy he saved us, by the washing of regeneration, and renewing of the Holy Ghost;—TITUS 3:5

  But ye are not in the flesh, but in the Spirit, if so be that the Spirit of God dwell in you. Now if any man have not the Spirit of Christ, he is none of his.—ROMANS 8:9

- **Renewal**—Your soul is being *renewed* by His daily work in your life.

  For which cause we faint not; but though our outward man perish, yet the inward man is renewed day by day.—2 CORINTHIANS 4:16

And be renewed in the spirit of your mind;—Ephesians 4:23

And have put on the new man, which is renewed in knowledge after the image of him that created him:—Colossians 3:10

- **Redemption**—Your body will one day be *redeemed*, and you will be given a new body which is waiting for you in Heaven.

Which is the earnest of our inheritance until the redemption of the purchased possession, unto the praise of his glory.—Ephesians 1:14

And not only they, but ourselves also, which have the firstfruits of the Spirit, even we ourselves groan within ourselves, waiting for the adoption, to wit, the redemption of our body.—Romans 8:23

And grieve not the holy Spirit of God, whereby ye are sealed unto the day of redemption.—Ephesians 4:30

This is huge! Most Christians think of salvation as something that happened in the past. In part, that's true—but it's a limited view. Yes, when you were saved, you were sealed in a moment; your new nature came to life; you were born into Jesus Christ. But that's just the first act of a larger work of God happening within you. It's the beginning point of the life-long maturing process of your new identity.

Let's break it down differently.

Step one—new birth. This happened the moment you were saved. Your faith in Jesus allowed Him to make you a new creature at the "spirit-level" of your being. This is a one-time, final, forever event. You have been born into God's family. This is significant because birth is a blood connection; it's irreversible. This means God has lovingly obligated Himself to you for all eternity. Your familial bond to God is absolute and irreversible.

But as many as received him, to them gave he power to become the sons of God, even to them that believe on his name:—JOHN 1:12

Step two—new mind. This is happening in you right now and for the rest of your earthly life. This is the renewing work of the Holy Spirit, changing and transforming you from the inside out, conforming you to the image of Jesus Christ. It's not something you can manufacture or perform on yourself. It's not something you can accurately measure or sense. It's something you must yield to and allow on a daily basis—by faith. You either allow it or prevent it. This is the center point of your daily struggle.

I beseech you therefore, brethren, by the mercies of God, that ye present your bodies a living sacrifice, holy, acceptable unto God, which is your reasonable service. And be not conformed to this world: but be ye transformed by the renewing of your mind, that ye may prove what is that good, and acceptable, and perfect, will of God.—ROMANS 12:1–2

Step three—new body. This is already created, waiting for you in Heaven. One day, your old body will be folded up like a tent (the Bible word is *tabernacle*), and you will put on a new body that is perfect and eternal. Right now your earthly body is decaying and dying, even though you try to take care of it. There's no reversing the curse of sin and the death that it has brought upon your body. But one day, you will shed that decaying sack of meat, and God will give you an incorruptible body— one that can never die, be sick, hurt, or broken.

Death is a fearful event to most men, but to the Christian, death is simply a step into a new body in eternity with Jesus. It's something to look forward to with hope and joy.

For we know that if our earthly house of this tabernacle were dissolved, we have a building of God, an house not made with hands, eternal in the heavens. For in this we groan, earnestly desiring to be clothed upon with our house which is from heaven:—2 CORINTHIANS 5:1–2

For this corruptible must put on incorruption, and this mortal must put on immortality.—1 CORINTHIANS 15:53

Beloved, now are we the sons of God, and it doth not yet appear what we shall be: but we know that, when he shall appear, we shall be like him; for we shall see him as he is.—1 JOHN 3:2

Who shall change our vile body, that it may be fashioned like unto his glorious body, according to the working whereby he is able even to subdue all things unto himself.—PHILIPPIANS 3:21

If you feel as though something about your salvation is *incomplete*, you're right! While you are not working *to be saved*, you are absolutely God's *work in progress*. You can never be unsaved or less saved, but you are truly undergoing a process of maturity that will take the rest of your life, and then it will finally culminate on the day you see Jesus face to face.

It's All about Jesus in Me

To summarize, your salvation was a *one-time* decision that began an *everyday* process and leads to a *someday* completion.

Jesus *regenerates* you instantly, *renews* you daily, and *redeems* you eventually. *Regeneration* is the moment of salvation. *Renewal* is your daily struggle of growth. *Redemption* is your eternal hope—that which you can anticipate and look forward to with patience. Your eternal destination is sealed and certain. Your daily growth is up to Jesus working in you, and your yielding to Him in faith. Your ultimate hope is the promise that one day, Jesus will redeem you from the struggle and give you a perfect, sinless body in a perfect forever.

This is why we began this chapter with this statement. "As a Christian—I'm not who I used to be; I'm not who I will be."

Until I see Jesus, I'm caught in between. This is, at times, a precarious and frustrating place to be.

Thankfully, I'm saved and safe. My sin was nailed to the cross of Jesus Christ. I don't need to fear any punishment or separation from God for my sin. But I'm trapped in a fleshly body that still struggles every day. I'm not who I was—thanks to Jesus. But I'm not yet who I will be—bummer!

I'm not who I was. Accept it. Appropriate it. You are not who you used to be. You are a new creature with a new Saviour and a new life. Much of it is unrealized, but all the potential is within you by God's grace.

I'm not who I will be. Accept it. Anticipate it. Real Christianity is a growing journey—a day-by-day walk with Jesus in which He is transforming and renewing me by His power, not my own.

This realization of being "in between" will either lead to hope or despair, and sometimes both in the same day! We'll explore the struggle in the next chapter.

Nine

The Struggle Within
Alive to God, Fighting the Flesh

My wife is a wonderful lady and my best friend, but she is absolutely directionally and geographically challenged.

A few years ago, she was taking some teen girls out to visit some recent youth group guests. Just imagine a minivan filled with giddy girls being driven by a directionally challenged mom, about to attempt basic navigation. This was a perfect storm.

Dana had just learned how to use her iPhone maps for directions, so she entered the address and started following the "blue dot" to the "red dot." Amazingly, it worked and they arrived at their first visit with no detours. Afterward, she entered the second address and began navigating toward the next "red dot." But halfway to the next visit, she somehow turned the phone upside down and transposed the dot locations in her mind.

A few moments later, after a lot of driving and navigating, she parked the van in front of the very home they had just visited fifteen minutes prior. She didn't realize what she had done and neither did the girls.

She looked at the house, and said, "I'm sure! This phone just took us all the way around town only to bring us right back to the same house! These girls live in the same home! We were just here!"

For a moment they were all in a foggy, murky place of intellectual confusion. Something wasn't right about this picture, but no one really knew what it was. The perplexity brought a few seconds of strange silence. But then, the light bulb came on and the whole group exploded into laughter. They couldn't wait to share the story with me when they arrived back at church.

Directionally Challenged, Disoriented, and Disillusioned

I must confess—as a Christian, I've faced many seasons when I was directionally challenged and disoriented on my spiritual journey. What began as a sweet relationship with Jesus eventually led to a place of distance and doubt. What began with *winning,* led to the nagging feeling of *losing*. What began with joy, led to despair and frustration.

I meet many Christians who are similarly disillusioned. The promise of being Christian has somehow broken down. It was "less than they expected." The hope found in Christ has been tarnished by the hurt of this present life. The "new nature" that was born at salvation hasn't fully emerged or matured, and the old self seems very alive and fighting for control.

If you don't identify with this yet, you will. Don't let it surprise you. Expect it.

One day you will find yourself tired of the struggle—tired of trying. You will think, "I'm not cut out for this like other people appear to be." You will come to a place of spiritual exhaustion. The hope you found in

Christ will seem to fade into weariness and failure. You'll find yourself in a fog of disillusionment and guilt.

You will probably think of giving up and walking away from Jesus and church. Or you will become tolerant of certain sins in your life, abusing grace, and giving up the fight.

This has happened to me more times than I can count. Early in my walk with Jesus it became clear—I don't know what I'm doing. I felt like I couldn't get it right, like I couldn't measure up to my new place in God's family. My faith in Jesus collided with my failure to live up to the name "Christian." I felt like I was nothing but a big disappointment to God—one of His "let downs" in the grand redemption of mankind.

Well, I'm a pretty tenacious guy, so I regrouped. I renewed my decisions and redoubled my efforts. Others around me seemed to be doing well in this thing called "the Christian life"—I can do this! This was a rededication of self-effort, not a renewal of dependence.

I just couldn't get it right. I couldn't get my *belief* in sync with my *behavior*, and all of it in sync with God's apparently very high expectations. I couldn't force "how I behaved" to be consistent with "what I believed."

I beat myself up constantly—certain that I deserved it. I shamed and guilted myself to sleep and determined to try harder tomorrow. I was sure that God was unhappy with me. Knowing Him was a joy, but trying to be everything He asked was a burden.

This is the negative side of being "in between"—it's the hard part of being a new creature in an old flesh waiting for the process of renewal and redemption to be completed. The process of growing was hard.

Basically, after my salvation, I made the mistake of trying to transform myself. I meant well, but was off track. I jumped onto a treadmill of "goodness" and tried to get myself into shape for Jesus. The treadmill was an exhausting attempt to make myself better for Him and do enough for

Him. But it was a deceptive detour from real Christianity. It prevented me from really knowing Him and enjoying Him, and it all but stopped me from growing in grace.

What Is Enough?

The concept of "enough" is a problem. Nothing could ever be *enough* if you're talking about behaving well and doing what Jesus deserves. How could you ever be, do, or achieve enough for an infinite Saviour who gave you His infinite grace? What could *you*—an imperfect, fallible being—*possibly offer* the God who has everything already? How could you ever love or worship God to the point that He says, "Okay—stop. That's enough. Thank you. You have arrived. I've had all the love and glory I deserve. You may now do something else."

The experience of "having so far to go" will overwhelm you if you let it. You will always look out on the horizon of your Christian walk and wonder if you've made any progress at all. You will see the vast distance of growth that stretches out before you and be very disheartened. Think about all that's left to learn, to do, to accomplish for Jesus. I'm getting discouraged just writing this!

It will all lead you to one of two responses.

First response, you could try harder. It's a mind game. The only way you could conclude that you can be or do "enough" is if you radically reduce the scale of expectation. You must massively downsize His holiness and upsize your own ability. You must underestimate the distance of "unrealized" growth and goodness and overestimate your own ability to "make it happen."

In this, you will create your own standard of measurement—which will always be almost reachable and slightly better than those around you. Then you will work your hardest to beat your own system. When you win, you will congratulate yourself and feel that God smiles. Trying harder only works if *you or others* set the standard and you succeed at *your own* standard.

Men don't set the standard—God does. And His standard is absolute perfection. Realizing this will set you back in discouragement. You haven't come as far as you thought. You haven't done as much as you estimated. There are still a billion miles of progress stretching out between you and perfection.

Second response, you could rest in Jesus. The scale of goodness that God expects is epically massive, and you are epically weak. The growth ahead is much bigger than you could ever achieve. No matter how good, how holy, how perfectly you behave; no matter how much you expend, serve, give, or sacrifice; no matter how hard you work or exhaust yourself, there will always be much more to do and much further to grow.

No matter how exceptional you attempt to be "for God," it always feels like a failed attempt to "jump to the moon." When it comes to growing, there will always be a greater distance ahead of you than behind you. It's just fact.

This will lead you to do one thing—*collapse.*

But here's the key. Will you collapse in *despair* or collapse in *hope*? Will you cast away your confidence, or will you cast yourself completely on Jesus? Will you despair of hope or depend upon Him?

Casting all your care upon him; for he careth for you.—1 PETER 5:7

Real Christianity is *designed* by God to *overwhelm* you to the point that you have only one option—to realize that He is enough and cast yourself upon Him in total dependence.

Jesus is enough.

This realization is the starting point of real growth in Jesus. Remember Peter? Absolute brokenness was the beginning of real usefulness. The end of self is the beginning of real Christianity.

As a new believer, you're in good company! The Bible was written to new believers! And the author of Hebrews addressed this process of despair when he was writing to new Christians.

> *But call to remembrance the former days, in which, after ye were illuminated, ye endured a great fight of afflictions. Cast not away therefore your confidence, which hath great recompence of reward. For ye have need of patience, that, after ye have done the will of God, ye might receive the promise. For yet a little while, and he that shall come will come, and will not tarry.*—HEBREWS 10:32, 35–37

Do you see it? He says, "Remember how life got harder right after you were saved? Don't lose hope or confidence. There is a huge payoff for being patient and faithful in this struggle. You *will* receive the promise! He *will* redeem you! Be patient and don't quit."

Here it is again from James, the brother of Jesus:

> *Be patient therefore, brethren, unto the coming of the Lord. Behold, the husbandman waiteth for the precious fruit of the earth, and hath long patience for it, until he receive the early and latter rain. Be ye also patient; stablish your hearts: for the coming of the Lord draweth nigh.*
> —JAMES 5:7–8

Struggling Christian

> *But I see another law in my members, warring against the law of my mind, and bringing me into captivity to the law of sin which is in my members.*—ROMANS 7:23

I'm a struggling Christian. My struggle is in its thirty-eighth year of *groaning*. And yes, everything I described earlier in this chapter characterizes my experiences and misadventures in my Christian life. These descriptors are my own raw feelings, played out on the bleeding edge of my own internal battles.

I've quit more than I can admit. You won't find a bigger loser, a greater "undeserver," a more proficient "Christian failure." And the longer I'm saved, the more I walk with Jesus, the more aware I become of what a "problem child" I really am. No matter how hard I've tried for over thirty-seven years, I can't get this "Christian life thing" straight! (At this point, picture me implanting my fingers in the shape of a "capital L" smack in the middle of my forehead!) Loser! That's me. That's all of us. Which is why our only hope is Jesus.

While being saved is the most awesome thing that ever happened to me, being a Christian is the most impossible thing I've ever attempted. It's a paradox of paradoxes—joyfully troublesome, blissfully burdensome, wonderfully hard.

The Christian life is a relationship with your Creator that will lead you into a fiery furnace to meet a faithful Friend, into a raging storm to discover a sovereign Saviour, into a whale's belly to find amazing grace, to a bloody cross to meet a suffering God, and into a deathly tomb to discover new life.

It's a relationship in which dying is living, losing is finding, surrendering is winning, and failure is not final—*ever!*

It's a journey where defeat is drowned in mercy and imperfection is shrouded in unconditional love. It's a life where only *destitution* is granted *deliverance,* only *ruin* is *redeemed,* and only *death* can be *resurrected.*

If you struggle as a Christian, if you are having a hard time "living the Christian life," congratulations on being exactly like every other Christian who ever lived! (Even those who pretend to have it all together.) If you are discouraged, frustrated, and ready to quit—you're normal. If you're hoping there's some utopian moment of victory out there somewhere, someday—you're not all that far from truth. That moment is out there. It's just not *now*. It's not *here*. Not yet.

> Which hope we have as an anchor of the soul, both sure and stedfast, and which entereth into that within the veil;—HEBREWS 6:19

For now, we groan. We wrestle, wait, endure, and rest. We fight forward in faith. These are the words Jesus used to describe our painful present. We earnestly desire that blissful joy we longed for the moment we trusted Christ. We crave the ultimate victory promised over sin. We long for that new body. We yearn for a struggle-free heart. We long for God's rescue to be complete—redemption to run its full course. Being suspended between *then* and *now* is just plain hard.

Yes, we're stuck in a struggle. The life of a bride before the wedding involves some waiting, some enduring, some weariness, even some frustration. But the dream of the wedding day—the promise of the Bride Groom, the hope of Heaven, overshadows all the grief.

Then outweighs *now*. Hope holds us together when all else pulls us apart.

Welcome to Normal

If you experience these up and down emotions—you're *normal*. It's woven into our human psyche to try to "measure up." But the gospel is the "good news" that you can't measure up and you don't have to. You don't need to "measure up." You need to cry "mercy." Biblical Christianity is an adventure in *lavish grace*—undeserved favor, unmerited love, unearned goodness.

We long for what is promised. A Saviour. Grace. Goodness. Abundant life. Hope. Heaven.

We dream of rescue and sigh for relief. We almost lose hope.

We long for the promise of *redemption*. But for now we find ourselves suspended between a serene someday and a painful present. We're not where we *were*, and we're not where we *want to be*.

This is real Christianity. This experience connects you with every disciple, every apostle, every great Bible Christian and first century believer. You are just like everybody else that ever walked with Jesus. Don't despair. Don't give up and walk away—it's all going somewhere in God's perfect plan!

Your struggle is merely evidence of one thing—*you need Him.*

The struggle may catch you by surprise. The ups and downs of walking with Jesus may sometimes drain the energy and joy from you. But it's all a part of real Christianity and daily life "in between" then and now. But Jesus is walking with you, and He makes the journey joyful in spite of the junk!

Understanding the Struggle

If you only remember one statement from this chapter, this is it: *God's good work in me goes on.*

But how? What's the significance of the struggle? And how does this struggle play into God's bigger picture?

God tells us much about it, and He uses our old friend Saul to get the point across. Remember Saul—Christian killer turned Jesus-follower? He became Paul, and he transparently shared his struggle with us.

First take note of his encouragement, *"Being confident of this very thing, that he which hath begun a good work in you will perform it until the day of Jesus Christ"* (Philippians 1:6).

Begin and end with *confidence* in Jesus—not fear, not anxiety, not despair. Have confidence and hope. You are accepted. You are a new creature. You are in Jesus.

Next, realize His good work is *always* happening in you. You may not see it, feel it, sense it, or understand it. But bank on it—Jesus is always performing a good work in you from now until you see Him. There will never be a moment when He quits working on you. There will never be a moment when you don't need to be worked on. You will never be *complete* until you see Him.

Many Christians lose hope and eventually quit because they don't understand this. They have never grasped that, through it all—the successes, the failures, and everything in between—Jesus is performing His good work within them.

The Apostle Paul walked every day with confidence in Jesus, but he also endured a daily struggle within himself. He put up with the same internal struggle that you do. But he didn't let it bring him to despair or hopelessness. He got it! I hope you will too!

Let's examine the three-fold struggle within.

The Inward Man—The New Me

Paul clearly identified his "new self" and the new desires that Jesus produced within him. In the verses below he explains the conflict between his inner desires and outward behavior.

> For that which I do I allow not: for what I would, that do I not; but what I hate, that do I. If then I do that which I would not, I consent unto the law that it is good. Now then it is no more I that do it, but sin that dwelleth in me. For I delight in the law of God after the inward man:—ROMANS 7:15–17, 22

That he would grant you, according to the riches of his glory, to be strengthened with might by his Spirit in the inner man; —Ephesians 3:16

And that ye put on the new man, which after God is created in righteousness and true holiness.—Ephesians 4:24

And have put on the new man, which is renewed in knowledge after the image of him that created him:—Colossians 3:10

God's Word uses these terms to identify this new nature within us: *the inward man, inner man, hidden man of the heart, the new man, new creature, His workmanship, put on the Lord Jesus, Christ in me, seal of the Spirit.*

This is the part of you that cheers you on and comes alive when listening to God's Word, reading a biblical book, participating in the mission of Christ, walking with Jesus personally, or serving others. This part of you stands up with delight when you are somehow magnifying Jesus with your life. This is the Spirit of God within you!

Get this—this is the REAL YOU!

God's Spirit infuses your new nature to *want* to do right, *want* to know God, and *want* to glorify Him. Your new nature *wants* to know Scripture, *wants* to serve Him, and *wants* to obey Him.

This is all good—but hold the thought. It's not so simple.

The Outward Man—My Old Self (Flesh)

In the next verses, Paul identified the flesh and sin that still plagued him, even though his sin nature was dead.

For I know that in me (that is, in my flesh,) dwelleth no good thing: for to will is present with me; but how to perform that which is good I find not. For the good that I would I do not: but the evil which I would not, that I do. Now if I do that I would not, it is no more I that do it, but sin that dwelleth in me. I find then a law, that, when I would do good, evil is present with me.—ROMANS 7:18–21

So then they that are in the flesh cannot please God. But ye are not in the flesh, but in the Spirit, if so be that the Spirit of God dwell in you. Now if any man have not the Spirit of Christ, he is none of his. And if Christ be in you, the body is dead because of sin; but the Spirit is life because of righteousness. But if the Spirit of him that raised up Jesus from the dead dwell in you, he that raised up Christ from the dead shall also quicken your mortal bodies by his Spirit that dwelleth in you.—ROMANS 8:8–11

But put ye on the Lord Jesus Christ, and make not provision for the flesh, to fulfil the lusts thereof.— ROMANS 13:14

God's Word uses these terms for the sin that plagues us after salvation: *flesh, works of the flesh, outward man, lusts of the flesh, sin in me, former lusts, sin reigning in your mortal body, deeds of the flesh, evil present with me, law of sin.*

This is *not* your sin nature. Your sin nature was crucified with Christ and replaced with a new nature. You can't have two natures. This is your flesh—the soul part of your mind, will, and emotions that have long been programmed toward sinful behavior. Think of it this way, your sin nature is dead, but your flesh doesn't know that yet.

It's like the time I took my son Larry out to shoot his rifle. Late in the day, we stumbled upon a rattlesnake. I'll spare you the whole story, but suffice it to say, after unloading about twenty rounds into that snake, it was completely dead. In spite of this, it continued to twist and slither for a solid twenty minutes. It was dead, but it's body didn't know it yet.

And so it is with the power of sin in your flesh. Your sin nature died, but your flesh doesn't know it yet. It's still grasping for control—

trying to hold you hostage to sinful habits and behavior. If the Apostle Paul struggled with this, you will too.

Since birth, you've lived "in flesh." Your flesh is your earthly mind and body and all of its natural bent on being self-sufficient. It's all the "software" that your sin nature installed on the hard drive of your mind. You've been well trained for a long time! You've been solidly programmed to sin. Your flesh brainwashed you!

But when you were saved, a new nature with the perfect mind of Christ came alive and began to write new programming onto the hard drive of your mind. God's Spirit desires to etch the mind of Jesus onto your heart. It's a life-long process of renewal—unlearning old ways and relearning new ways in Christ, all by God's grace.

Your old ways of thinking, acting, and living will gradually be rewritten by God's Spirit, if you allow it. He will renew your mind and create new responses, new vocabulary, new attitudes, new purposes, and new behaviors. It's a wonderful process, but at times, the war gets wearying.

The War in the Middle

In the verse below, Paul explains the war going on between his new nature and his old flesh. This is why the Christian life is a struggle that requires patient endurance.

> But I see another law in my members, warring against the law of my mind, and bringing me into captivity to the law of sin which is in my members. O wretched man that I am! who shall deliver me from the body of this death? I thank God through Jesus Christ our Lord...
> —ROMANS 7:23–25

> For which cause we faint not; but though our outward man perish, yet the inward man is renewed day by day.—2 CORINTHIANS 4:16

This I say then, Walk in the Spirit, and ye shall not fulfil the lust of the flesh. For the flesh lusteth against the Spirit, and the Spirit against the flesh: and these are contrary the one to the other: so that ye cannot do the things that ye would. But if ye be led of the Spirit, ye are not under the law.—GALATIANS 5:16–18

In these verses we see a war raging. It's a battle for the control of your heart and behavior, and it's being fought between the flesh and the Spirit on the battlefield of your mind. The flesh desires to bring you into captivity to sin and self. God's Spirit desires to renew your mind as you grow in grace.

God also calls this the "fruit of the Spirit": *"For the fruit of the Spirit is in all goodness and righteousness and truth"* (Ephesians 5:9). In other words, this isn't something you can produce on your own or manufacture by self-will or effort. This is the organic, natural outflow of allowing God's Spirit to rule your heart. It's not a process you *force;* it's a process you *allow.* The best version of you is the new you under the control of the Holy Spirit of God. The worst version of you is you under the control of the flesh. Every day, you are led and controlled by one of the two, and it all depends upon who you allow to rule.

Know ye not, that to whom ye yield yourselves servants to obey, his servants ye are to whom ye obey; whether of sin unto death, or of obedience unto righteousness?—ROMANS 6:16

Every moment, you must choose who you are following in life—your flesh or God's Spirit. This sounds like you must lose your individual identity, but that's not true. You are never more fully who God designed you to be than when you are fully surrendered to God's Spirit. When God is ruling your heart, He lives out the character of Jesus through your unique personality. He maximizes your strengths and minimizes your weaknesses. It's not an exercise in being "just like every other Christian." It's an exercise in fully becoming who Jesus uniquely created you to be.

The Blessings of the War Within

It's strange to think that there are actually some blessings from this struggle. That might sound bizarre, but God's Word reveals it. Be very clear—this struggle is a part of God's design of the Christian journey. When God saved you, He could have made all three parts of salvation happen instantly. New nature, new mind, new body—all in the moment of faith! How cool would that have been?

He chose otherwise. He designed the work of salvation to be three parts that unfold over a lifetime. This is His plan, and in many ways, it's beyond our understanding. But Scripture gives us insight to how God uses this struggle to accomplish His ultimate purpose.

Here are some ways the struggle brings blessing:

The struggle highlights God's grace—turning bad things into good. It's called reconciliation. In the same chapter where God details the struggle of yielding to the Spirit, He says this:

> *And we know that all things work together for good to them that love God, to them who are the called according to his purpose.*—ROMANS 8:28

The struggle teaches me to walk in the Spirit. It keeps me dependent upon God and yielding to His Spirit. It compels me to daily ask Him to fill and control my life!

> *This I say then, Walk in the Spirit, and ye shall not fulfil the lust of the flesh.*—GALATIANS 5:16

> *And be not drunk with wine, wherein is excess; but be filled with the Spirit;*—EPHESIANS 5:18

The struggle keeps me growing in my relationship with Jesus. My vulnerability and susceptibility to sin compels me to walk with Him personally. It keeps me needy. It calls me to read His Word, attend a Bible-believing church, and fellowship with Christian friends. Why? Because I have to? No. Because I'm required to? No. Because that's what good Christians do? No. Because I love Him and need Him.

These things are the product of loving Him. That love makes me desire growth in grace and obey God's Word. The Christian life is not a *have to* life—it's a *want to* life!

> *But grow in grace, and in the knowledge of our Lord and Saviour Jesus Christ. To him be glory both now and for ever. Amen.*—2 PETER 3:18

The struggle reveals the high value of His work within me. The struggle is an indicator that God's Word is true and there is something at stake in not walking with Jesus. Spiritual warfare is evidence of a high-stakes, high-value part of life—a spiritual dimension to life in which there is much to lose to sin, and much to gain in Jesus.

> *And let us not be weary in well doing: for in due season we shall reap, if we faint not.*—GALATIANS 6:9

> *Esteeming the reproach of Christ greater riches than the treasures in Egypt: for he had respect unto the recompence of the reward.* —HEBREWS 11:26

The struggle keeps me hoping for Heaven and home. It's easy to become complacent and satisfied with this short life. God has something much better in store for you, and He calls you to set your affection on Himself and Heaven. He calls you to live for a higher hope. The war keeps me longing for home.

Set your affection on things above, not on things on the earth.
—Colossians 3:2

The struggle keeps me magnifying Jesus. How could my Christian struggle glorify Jesus? Through faith. Faith is what Jesus acknowledges in your life, and your faith in the struggle—your absolute refusal to give up or to quit trusting—brings Him glory. Your steadfastness through the fight will magnify Him.

> *But without faith it is impossible to please him: for he that cometh to God must believe that he is, and that he is a rewarder of them that diligently seek him.*—Hebrews 11:6

The struggle keeps me authentic in Christian relationships. Christianity is often plagued with fakery and pretense. We descend into political games of comparing ourselves and judging each other. It's sad, but common—even in the early church—though the Bible clearly teaches against it.

In every case, these games would go away if we would be authentic about the struggles of our hearts. About the time I want to accuse or blame someone else, I remember how broken I am, and suddenly I don't feel so "high and mighty."

> *Who art thou that judgest another man's servant? to his own master he standeth or falleth. Yea, he shall be holden up: for God is able to make him stand.*—Romans 14:4

> *Confess your faults one to another, and pray one for another, that ye may be healed. The effectual fervent prayer of a righteous man availeth much.*—James 5:16

The struggle keeps me small so He can be big. The Christian life is a downward cycle of continually humbling myself before God and others. My struggle keeps me familiar with my weakness and brokenness. The longer I struggle, the smaller I become in my own estimation and the larger God's grace becomes! This is healthy as long as it compels *dependence* and not *discouragement*.

We all tend to be glory hogs. Even as we grow in grace, we measure ourselves and glory in our own goodness. We think highly of our progress. We compare ourselves to others. It's a game that robs God of the credit He alone deserves.

> *I am the vine, ye are the branches: He that abideth in me, and I in him, the same bringeth forth much fruit: for without me ye can do nothing.* —JOHN 15:5

> *He must increase, but I must decrease.*—JOHN 3:30

God's Good Work Goes On

There are many days when I'm tired of the struggle within. I get tired of the hard side of the Christian journey. You will too. But on those days, I find the struggle is often a function of my own pride or false expectations. The burden is self-imposed or others-imposed. It's never Jesus-imposed. Jesus invites me to rest in Him.

> *Come unto me, all ye that labour and are heavy laden, and I will give you rest. Take my yoke upon you, and learn of me; for I am meek and lowly in heart: and ye shall find rest unto your souls. For my yoke is easy, and my burden is light.*—MATTHEW 11:28–30

Jesus doesn't expect me to *do* the good work in me. He is already doing it. Usually when I'm discouraged it's because I've misappropriated this truth. I've taken matters into my own hands. I'm trying to *make* fruit grow or *force* maturity to happen. All of my self-effort sets me up for failure and discouragement.

Then, Jesus almost audibly whispers to my tired heart, "Are you going to do this or am I?"

I usually respond, "Jesus, I love You—so I want to do this for You! I ought to be better. I need to try harder. I should be a better Christian by now."

Again He says, "Are you going to do this or am I? If you are, then I can't. If you will rest and yield to Me—be still—I will do the work."

Finally, and a bit resentfully at times, I give in. Self dies and the Spirit takes over. My flesh (masquerading in a spiritual cover) wanted to be good for Jesus. My flesh wanted the credit for making myself "like Jesus."

God's plan is one of yielding—total dependence. When you fail— He picks you up. When you succeed—He gets the credit. Through it all— every success and every struggle—He is doing a good work in you.

The Christian life is a *wonderful* life! Yes. The Christian life is also a *warring* life! Yes.

There are two critical things that make the war bearable.

The first—knowing that one day, you win!

The second—knowing that through it all, God's good work goes on!

Brethren, I count not myself to have apprehended: but this one thing I do, forgetting those things which are behind, and reaching forth unto those things which are before, I press toward the mark for the prize of the high calling of God in Christ Jesus.—PHILIPPIANS 3:13–14

Ten

Game Plan
A Biblical Strategy for a Winning Christian Life

Emotional scars are still evident from my eighth grade football season. The details are bloody and messy, but suffice it to say, I was the worst junior varsity football player in the history of humanity. In my first game, coach put me in the game during the second half. My position was defensive end. If you had put a gun to my head and asked me "What is the job of a defensive end?" I would not be alive to write these words today.

Just a few short moments after getting into the game, the opposing team ran two touchdowns around my end of the defense. I was oblivious.

People hated me. My teammates cursed me. My coach nearly ripped my head off my body when he grabbed my face mask. And he nearly bit his own tongue in two with his seething anger. My parents, sitting in the grandstands, covered their heads in sackcloth and ashes.

A few games later, I was brought onto the varsity "special teams." I have no clue what the coaches were thinking. This time, it was homecoming for our school, so the entire state was coming out to watch me humiliate myself and all who knew me. On the opening kickoff, I had a sickening sense that this ball was coming straight to me. Though I was in the front line, I just had a haunting feeling that this kicker was going to botch the kick—perhaps God's Spirit was warning me to get ready.

Seconds later, it was as though reality went into slow motion as the kicker flubbed the kick and launched the ball into a small arc that placed me directly at the end of the rainbow! I panicked. I should have run for my life. In the flash of a few seconds, my short life raced before my eyes. My brain quickly calculated the weight of the older, bigger varsity players, now headed my direction. I knew I was about to be pulverized and possibly permanently disabled. My dreams of a future, a family, a ministry—they all evaporated in an instant. This was the end, I just knew it.

Then the ball fell into my arms—and then straight through my arms. It bobbled between my feet. I scrambled—not knowing whether to grab the ball or save my life. The defense was bearing down fast. I grasped and clawed for the ball while watching the wall of angry defenders pouring in my direction. They were foaming at the mouth, growling—my death was imminent.

Finally, unable to get control, I just sat on the ball, and then rolled over on it—and just in time. The defense piled on top of me, fighting for the football. I held on for dear life—even though dear life was quickly leaving my crushed lungs!

In that moment I wanted to die. My friends and family were all warming their hands by a fire and denying knowing me with oaths and cursing. Again, my teammates were screaming at me. My coach just put his head in his hands and groaned. It was all very, very sad—and scarring.

You know the problem? I didn't get the game plan—at least not at that age. It was all so new and confusing—I really didn't know what I needed to know. And what I knew simply made me dangerous to myself. I didn't know that what I did actually wasn't such a bad response to my circumstances. I actually did the *right thing,* even by professional football standards.

I *thought* I was supposed to catch the ball and run a touchdown. I was wrong. Nobody but me had this expectation. In actual football strategy, when a frontline kickoff-receiving-team player is about to receive a flubbed kickoff, his primary objective is to *retain possession* for the team. Whether he catches the ball, falls on the ball, or in my case, sits on the ball—if he retains possession, he is *successful!* On top of that, his team has great field position for a kick off.

Truth be told, we should have been *celebrating* my sitting! We retained possession of the ball, and my team had great field position. If a receiver had caught the ball at the ten-yard-line and run it all the way back to the forty-yard-line, we would have been celebrating!

I did the right thing—but it surely felt wrong. It wasn't pretty. It didn't look heroic. It was rather unathletic and awkward in appearance, but it was *right*. Until this writing, this has never occurred to me. All my life I've lived under this shadow of embarrassment—the emotional scars of that moment—and today I'm finally free!

Hopefully, this book will have the same impact on your walk with Jesus. Maybe you have expectations that nobody has, but you! Perhaps God doesn't even have your expectations. Maybe you've placed upon yourself a burden that Jesus is trying to get you to lay down.

Often, our frustration or disappointment in Christianity is that we don't get the game plan. We don't understand how it's supposed to be lived out daily—and so we berate and bully ourselves over things that God doesn't. We impose expectations upon ourselves that God doesn't. Jesus already fulfilled all the expectations.

We live for years thinking we are failures, but in God's game plan, we're normal Christians, living out real Christianity.

Resolving Paul's Confusion

Sometimes I want to ask the Apostle Paul, "So which are you? Are you a saint? Or are you the chief of sinners? Are you a wretched man or a new creature? Or are you just confused, because these statements seem contradictory in the extreme?"

These things seem conflicted, until you know the game plan and understand the reality. In truth, Paul's answer to these questions would be, "Yes."

"Yes, I'm a sinner. Yes, I'm a saint. Yes, I'm a wretched man. Yes, I'm a new creature. It's all true, and God accepts me absolutely as I am."

My next question would be, "Then what is God's response? If you're a wretched man, it seems like God would reject you. If you're a new creature, it seems like God would bless you."

His answer would simply be, "Grace. What is God's response to my wretchedness? Grace. How was I made a new creature? Grace. Amazing, unlimited, inexhaustible, undeserved grace!"

My final question would be, "Paul, what's the answer? How is God going to minimize your wretchedness and maximize your new creature? Seems like you're a hardworking guy, but you always say that Jesus is living through you. What is God's game plan for taking you forward? Is it work or rest? Is it effort or surrender? Does God change you because you try? Or because you stop trying?"

Again Paul's answer would be, "Yes. Grace."

These are the questions we're going to explore in this chapter. Since we know that God isn't merely modifying our behavior, what is the game plan of Christianity?

Once I'm saved and undergoing the process of renewal, what does the daily walk look like practically? What am I supposed to do? And how am I supposed to think?

Look at what God says:

I am crucified with Christ: nevertheless I live; yet not I, but Christ liveth in me: and the life which I now live in the flesh I live by the faith of the Son of God, who loved me, and gave himself for me.—GALATIANS 2:20

God desires for your relationship with Him to show up on the outside—in your behavior. He intends to change you, both inside and out. He calls you to live differently than before salvation. But it's all His work *in* you, not your work *for* Him. It's a matter of obedient surrender to the work of the Holy Spirit. It's a matter of *allowing* the work of God, not attempting to *force* it with clenched fists and gritted teeth. Simply put, it's a response to God's grace.

Living for Jesus or Jesus Living through Me?

Wherefore, my beloved, as ye have always obeyed, not as in my presence only, but now much more in my absence, work out your own salvation with fear and trembling. For it is God which worketh in you both to will and to do of his good pleasure.—PHILIPPIANS 2:12–13

It's easy to start trying to live *for* Jesus rather than living *in* Jesus! These are very different things. One is performance driven; the other is Spirit-led. God teaches us in the verses above that His work within produces two things—the *will* and the *ability* to obey: "*For it is God which worketh in you both to will and to do of his good pleasure*" (Philippians 2:13). The *will* is my inner desire, and *to do* is the ability to act and behave God's way. Any good that takes place within you, or any good that flows from you, will be a direct result of God's grace.

Will you do good work after salvation? Sure—but it isn't to be done in self-dependence. It's not of yourself or your own strength. Your good works will be an exercise in utter dependence.

Going forward, your effort in the Christian life will either be self-driven—in which case it will be fruitless and phony, or it will be Jesus-driven—your yielding to Jesus—in which case He will produce authentic fruit to His glory.

The hard part is knowing the difference. Fake fruit and authentic fruit appear the same on the surface. The external behavior looks similar but flows from different sources. Like Paul said, "I live, but it's not me—Jesus lives through me."

The easiest thing to do in the Christian life is to get off the *grace path* and onto the *works path*. It's easy to start worshiping "good works" more than worshiping Jesus—the Author and Source of the good works. It's easy to try to please Him in self-effort rather than yield to Him in self-abandonment. It's easy to try to do right but in my own strength and flesh. In this, my effort becomes:

- Self-dependence not Jesus-dependence
- Self-glory not God's glory
- Sinfulness not holiness
- Flesh not faith
- Me not Jesus

Killing my self-dependence is a work only God can do. Through patient purging and chastening, He walks with us every day, dealing with us as His children, and cultivating our hearts toward holiness. He lovingly reveals our pride. He allows our struggles to humble us. He allows failure to knock us down so He can pick us up, brush us off, restore us in grace, and help us go forward in renewed dependence upon Jesus.

The Death of Flesh

This is all about the *death of flesh*. It's a lifelong, slow, and at times, painful death. Flesh doesn't go down without a fight. Be sure, flesh will lose, but it's going to take some time. You can fight forward in total confidence— flesh *will* lose! It's *guaranteed*. But it dies kicking and screaming.

It's impossible for *me* to evaluate whether *you* are performing *for* Jesus or living *through* Jesus. No man can determine that from an outside view. (And beware of a man who tries.) No man can discern the thoughts and motives of another man's heart. I can barely discern my *own* heart. Just when I think my motives are finally pure, God reveals otherwise.

Ambition to *do* or *be* for God is a mixed bag—it can be pure or proud. Ambition is not always *prideful*, but it is not always *pure* either— and most of the time it's some of *both!* Untangling self from Spirit is a grace process that only God can do. Again, think of Peter and the purification process that Jesus allowed him to go through.

Perhaps you still feel like a beginner. You still feel discouraged that you lose your struggle sometimes—or a lot of times. You feel condemned by your own conscience.

If you're not careful you'll start to live *for* Jesus rather than live *in* Jesus!

There's really nothing you alone can do *for* Him. But there's a lot you can do *through* Him. There's a lot He can do *in* you and *through* you!

Winning is **in** Jesus not **for** Jesus

For in him we live, and move, and have our being; as certain also of your own poets have said, For we are also his offspring.—ACTS 17:28

I can do all things through Christ which strengtheneth me.
—PHILIPPIANS 4:13

I am the vine, ye are the branches: He that abideth in me, and I in him, the same bringeth forth much fruit: for without me ye can do nothing.
—JOHN 15:5

Not that we are sufficient of ourselves to think any thing as of ourselves; but our sufficiency is of God;—2 CORINTHIANS 3:5

And he said unto me, My grace is sufficient for thee: for my strength is made perfect in weakness. Most gladly therefore will I rather glory in my infirmities, that the power of Christ may rest upon me.
—2 CORINTHIANS 12:9

These verses and many more teach the single big take away from this chapter: *Winning is in Jesus not for Jesus!*

Live *for* Him—this could be me in self-effort trying to impress or win Him! This is me trying to *make* myself holy. This is all about my glory, not His. Even when I say, "This is all to the glory of God"—it can be stated with a subtle, "I did this all for Him. Yay, me! Am I not *amazing?!*"

Any part of "Yay, me" in your good works boils down to self-glory— even when you mask it with spiritual terms. This is subtle and sneaks up on us. I am incredibly adept at masking self-glory and self-works in spiritual terms. In words, God gets the glory. In heart and intent, it's more like, "God must be really amazed at how much I glorify Him! He's lucky to have me. He's surely getting a lot more glory because of me."

This is a spiritual dead-end road, because it makes me big and Him small. It reduces the scale of goodness. It overestimates my ability. It reduces grace and God. It takes the spotlight off of Jesus and places it onto me and my contrived spirituality.

Living *in* Him—this is me in total dependence, letting Jesus live through me. This is Him growing me in holiness. It really is all His work and all His glory. This is my discovering how weak, broken, and messy I am. Rather than quitting in despair, I cast myself in absolute weakness upon the grace of God. I collapse into His strength and sufficiency. My minimal effort is offered in faith as a "living sacrifice" (Romans 12:1). I realize my self-work adds up to nothing. My ability and goodness don't even register on God's scale.

This is my *yielding* in total surrender to Jesus. It's my realizing His Spirit will transform me if I will submit to Him. It's a faith thing, not a feeling. It's not experiential—it's factual, as a result of faith and surrender.

This is a much needed, massive perspective shift regarding real Christianity. Get it?

Everything you do in the Christian life is either about you trying to grace Jesus, or Jesus trying to grace you!

God didn't save you so you could grace Him. He saved you so He could grace you.

He wants it all, in totality, to be about Jesus and His grace in you. He desires and deserves 100 percent of the glory—all the credit. He wants Jesus to be magnified, not you.

Jesus doesn't need your grace, *you need His!* But somehow, after salvation, we take matters into our own hands and start living like we believe we can grace God with our favors, our goodness, our righteousness. We treat salvation like a steroid that made us "able to get it done for Him." In reality, salvation is not a modest power boost. It's a total rescue from absolute destitution and utter helplessness.

God's Simple Game Plan

Like my misunderstanding of the kickoff team's game plan, my Christian living game plan was skewed. Early on, I depended upon *my* resources, *my* strategy, and *my* effort. Yet, over time, God chastened me, broke me down through the struggle, and revealed to me my absolute dependence upon His grace. I understood dependence in theory, but in practice I was often living independently. This continues to be a struggle to this very day. It's easy to default back into self-dependence!

God's game plan for real Christianity goes against everything we would naturally think. We default to works of righteousness. Our flesh wants glory. We want to compare ourselves with others and measure ourselves as successful. Which is why God's game plan has nothing to do with self-righteousness and all to do with His grace and goodness working in us.

His game plan is not a strategy of working hard, but depending more as we obey in response to His grace.

Independence says, "Jesus, look at how mature I've become. I must be really good in Your eyes!" (This magnifies self.)

Dependence says, "Jesus, without You I can do nothing. I need You to live through me, in me, and in spite of me!" (This magnifies Jesus.)

> *I am crucified with Christ: nevertheless I live; yet not I, but Christ liveth in me: and the life which I now live in the flesh I live by the faith of the Son of God, who loved me, and gave himself for me.*—GALATIANS 2:20

In the big picture, real Christianity is a simple game plan. Daily living breaks down to three simple components:

First, Love Jesus

> *So when they had dined, Jesus saith to Simon Peter, Simon, son of Jonas, lovest thou me more than these? He saith unto him, Yea, Lord; thou knowest that I love thee. He saith unto him, Feed my lambs.*
> —JOHN 21:15

And thou shalt love the Lord thy God with all thy heart, and with all thy soul, and with all thy mind, and with all thy strength: this is the first commandment.—MARK 12:30

If ye love me, keep my commandments.—JOHN 14:15

The greatest thing you can "do" as a Christian is love Jesus. If you ever hear anyone cheapen or diminish the love of Jesus, run for your life. Love for Christ is the greatest motivation for every other moral behavior or good work. Anything less than *love* is a cheap substitute for real Christianity.

Looking back at Peter's story, it's critical to note that Jesus foretold Peter's failure, repentance, and restoration. He was planning to use it for good, to reveal to Peter his own weakness and propensity to love self more than Saviour!

And the Lord said, Simon, Simon, behold, Satan hath desired to have you, that he may sift you as wheat: But I have prayed for thee, that thy faith fail not: and when thou art converted, strengthen thy brethren.
—LUKE 22:31–32

And when failure actually occurred, it was not merely a breakdown of behavior. It was a breakdown of love. Jesus didn't ask Peter, "Why did you do those things? Why did you deny and forsake Me?" He asked Peter, "Do you love Me?" Convicting.

Jesus didn't badger, judge, or bring the hammer down on Peter. He simply asked about his love.

God could motivate you in any way He chooses. He could leverage pain, manipulate circumstances, obligate you with debt, force you with authority. Grace bypasses all of these lesser motivations and calls you to the highest motivation known to any relationship—love.

Any breakdown in your walk with Jesus is a love breakdown. Every time I sin, I'm choosing to love something more than Jesus.

Some Christians fail to see love and grace as motivators. They prefer law and discipline to *legislate* behavior, rather than grace to *motivate* behavior.

They are afraid that, if they (or others) embrace the grace path, it becomes a license to sin—a free pass for tolerance of bad behavior. They fear if they teach or preach unconditional acceptance, Christians will "do less" for Jesus and for the church. This is a gross underestimation of the power of God's grace and a gross overestimation of human ability to leverage lesser motivations toward behavioral goodness. It's also a recipe for great discouragement in your relationship with Jesus and your church.

Think of it this way. The highest quality of my marriage relationship with Dana is *love*. Our love for Jesus, my love for her, and her love for me is what holds us together. Love is what motivates us to forgive, to care, to serve, and to cherish each other. Being Dana's husband involves a lot of good behavior, but not *merely behavior*. Love that motivates behavior is what makes a great marriage.

All the good stuff of our marriage is driven by love. Though we are legally bound, though we are biblically obligated, though we share children and living arrangements, none of these things motivate us to stay together. Love for Jesus and for each other is our singular motivation.

What if I focused on mastering the behaviors of a good husband? What if I exhausted myself in service to her—doing laundry, cleaning the house, fueling her car—but it wasn't driven by love? She would have a servant, but not a husband. My good works would be empty and unfulfilling. Eventually, I would be exhausted and she would be distressed. The relationship would break. No amount of personal discipline or effort will produce what love can produce.

Good behaviors *alone* don't make a good Christian any more than they make a good husband. Love makes both! Love motivates behaviors that produce health. That's why Jesus called a hard working church back to Himself in Revelation 2.

Nevertheless I have somewhat against thee, because thou hast left thy first love.—REVELATION 2:4

Real Christianity is an experience in lavish grace that calls forth lavish love. The bigger and more extravagant I understand God's grace to be (the more accurately I see God's unconditional love) the more it deeply motivates me to LOVE Him. Grace wins my heart. Grace captivates me, compels me, and inspires me to love Him with all my heart, soul, mind, and strength!

The grace of God produces greater love for God, which in turn motivates me to repent when I fail, to walk away from lesser loves (sin), and to worship Him with my whole heart and life. It motivates, compels, and constrains me to grow in grace and holiness—by His power, not my own.

For the love of Christ constraineth us....—2 CORINTHIANS 5:14

For the grace of God that bringeth salvation hath appeared to all men, Teaching us that, denying ungodliness and worldly lusts, we should live soberly, righteously, and godly, in this present world;—TITUS 2:11–12

Or despisest thou the riches of his goodness and forbearance and longsuffering; not knowing that the goodness of God leadeth thee to repentance?—ROMANS 2:4

The first question you face in every sin struggle, every flesh struggle is simply, "Do I love Jesus?" This trumps every other kind of law, rule, or standard. As you grow in love with God, you will *want* to keep His commands and honor His name. You will *want* to glorify Him through godly choices and daily lifestyle.

Remember, real Christianity is not a *have to* life, it's a *want to* life! Why? Because of love!

Every time I have tried to motivate or discipline myself toward holy behavior, two things have happened. First, I have failed. Somewhere, in my self-effort, there's a breakdown. Second, I have underestimated the power of love and grace. Whatever I'm using to motivate myself is smaller, less powerful, and less genuine than the real love that God's grace produces.

Think of it this way. There are two big motivations for obedience—love or law. Grace or obligation. Law is "have to." Love is "want to." Grace doesn't motivate you to disobey or live carnally. That would be a massive perversion of grace and a gross misunderstanding of what Jesus did on the cross. That would turn Christianity into mere selfish exploitation of God and grace. A true understanding of grace and the gospel—real Christianity—will completely reorientate your values, your motives, and your loves. You will grow "out of love" with sin and "more in love" with Jesus. You will be compelled by His grace to obey Him, to serve Him, to honor Him in your life and choices—all because of your love for Him and His work of grace in your heart.

You will not be a slave to your sin, nor will you be the hostage of God's laws. It's a different economy altogether. It's a love economy. You live in love with God, and that deeply drives all other behavior and devotion.

Loving Jesus is the first and foremost value in God's game plan.

Second, Walk with Jesus

Abide in me, and I in you. As the branch cannot bear fruit of itself,
except it abide in the vine; no more can ye, except ye abide in me. I
am the vine, ye are the branches: He that abideth in me, and I in him,
the same bringeth forth much fruit: for without me ye can do nothing.
—JOHN 15:4–5

This I say then, Walk in the Spirit, and ye shall not fulfil the lust of the flesh.—Galatians 5:16

Relationships are made strong through time and attention. Relationships grow weak by neglect and distance. So it is in your relationship with Jesus. He invites you to yield to Him, to abide in Him, to walk with Him—and this relationship changes you. He changes you as you walk with Him.

As a believer, your love for Jesus should compel you to spend time with Him. He says it this way in Revelation 3:

Behold, I stand at the door, and knock: if any man hear my voice, and open the door, I will come in to him, and will sup with him, and he with me.—Revelation 3:20

Jesus says, "I'm waiting to 'sup' with you." That literally means to sit down and eat a meal together. When Dana and I really want to connect, there's nothing we enjoy more than going out for a meal. So, your Saviour invites you to know Him and enjoy Him in this same way.

When Jesus saved you, He didn't hire an employee, contract for services, or redeem you for forced labor. He rescued you, adopted you, and renewed you to Himself as His child. He is your Father—perfect, loving, gracious in every way. He wants you to *know* Him.

Real Christianity is an intimate, loving relationship with Jesus. The more time you spend with Him, the more you will love Him. The more you love Him, the more you will yield to His grace and goodness. The more you yield, the more He will change you. Your heart will change. Your love will grow. And your behavior will follow. After five or ten years of loving and walking with Jesus, you will be a very different person—all because of His grace. It will sneak up on you! You won't sense it, feel it, or be able to measure. But years later, the changes will be undeniably evident.

It's *in* Him and *through* Him, not *for* Him!

Loving Jesus leads to walking with Jesus, which leads to step three:

Third, Depend upon Jesus

Likewise reckon ye also yourselves to be dead indeed unto sin, but alive unto God through Jesus Christ our Lord. Let not sin therefore reign in your mortal body, that ye should obey it in the lusts thereof. Neither yield ye your members as instruments of unrighteousness unto sin: but yield yourselves unto God, as those that are alive from the dead, and your members as instruments of righteousness unto God.
—ROMANS 6:11–13

I beseech you therefore, brethren, by the mercies of God, that ye present your bodies a living sacrifice, holy, acceptable unto God, which is your reasonable service. And be not conformed to this world: but be ye transformed by the renewing of your mind, that ye may prove what is that good, and acceptable, and perfect, will of God.—ROMANS 12:1–2

After my cancer diagnosis, doctors basically took over my life. All of my priorities shifted. My values were suddenly radically altered. Survival was in question; therefore, all other priorities had to take a backseat to *survival.*

Strangely, there was nothing I could personally do to change my health diagnosis—except *yield.* I couldn't heal my cancer. Exercise, diet, vitamins, rest—none of these healthy things would have stopped cancer from growing. I couldn't command cancer to die or healthy cells to be born. I couldn't *will* myself into health. The death of cancer and the renewal of my cells required something well beyond my power.

So the medical world invaded all privacy, dignity, and personal priorities. You might say they demanded that I *yield my body as a living sacrifice!*

About seven weeks after diagnosis, my doctor instructed me to show up at the chemo room. Begrudgingly and fearfully, I did exactly what he told me. When I arrived, a friendly nurse welcomed me and instructed me to have a seat in one of several large green chairs. A few moments later she instructed me to roll up my shirt sleeve and yield my arm, whereupon she inserted an IV and began to administer chemotherapy chemicals into my bloodstream. God used those noxious chemicals to do something in my body that I couldn't do on my own. For this reason, I'm alive today to write these words.

Honestly, there is no way I could take credit for killing cancer. All I did was show up. I *yielded*. I presented my body for someone else to do the work.

This is real Christianity. There's a work in you that you cannot do, and if you try, you're going to fail. The good news is, Jesus is ready to do that work. The only thing you can "do" to facilitate the process is *yield*—present yourself to Him, depend upon His control and His power. His grace is the supernatural resource at work in you, and yielding to Him is the act of your conscious will to allow transformation.

As you present your body and yield to Him—He renews your mind, He changes your heart, He transforms your life.

Love Jesus, *walk* with Jesus, *depend* upon Jesus—that's God's simple game plan. Day by day, for the rest of your life, this relationship moves forward by *love*, is enjoyed in a *daily walk*, and produces personal change through *dependence*.

Is there more to it? Sure. There's a lot to learn. But ultimately, it boils down to those simple truths—*love, walk, depend*. Stay in love with Jesus. Keep walking with Him. Keep renewing your dependence—yielding. He will do the rest, and He will get the credit!

Dana and I have been in love for over twenty-seven years. We've had a lot of ups and downs in our relationship. There have been times we've both been disappointed or frustrated with each other. But when we were first married, we expected that there would be growth. We knew we needed to grow in love.

While Jesus is perfect, He knows you aren't. He knows you have a lot of growing to do—and He's already doing that work. The road ahead is a fight. It's a struggle. He knows that. You're going to be prone to wander and falter. He knows that, too.

More than that, the road ahead is a relationship! You are His child. He is your Father. You have all of His unconditional love and inexhaustible grace.

Keep *loving* Jesus. Keep *walking* with Jesus. Keep *depending* upon Jesus.

Let Him do the rest!

4

PART FOUR

Real Hope

Eleven

Failing Forward
Understanding Inexhaustible Grace

After accepting Jesus as Saviour, I set out to "become better for God." My motives were right, but my theology was wrong. Jesus sets us free from the penalty of sin immediately—*regeneration*. He sets us free from the power of sin gradually—*renewal*. And He sets us free from the presence of sin eventually—*redemption*. Regeneration, sanctification, redemption—this is the three-fold gospel that we've already studied. Therefore, my expectations to *immediately* conquer sin and the flesh were unrealistic.

Over and over again, I tried harder, only to discover that the harder I tried, the more I focused on the struggle and not on Jesus. The more I focused on the struggle, the harder it became. This is why God's game plan is not for you to focus on the struggle, but on Jesus.

Wherefore seeing we also are compassed about with so great a cloud of witnesses, let us lay aside every weight, and the sin which doth so easily beset us, and let us run with patience the race that is set before us, Looking unto Jesus the author and finisher of our faith; who for the joy that was set before him endured the cross, despising the shame, and is set down at the right hand of the throne of God. For consider him that endured such contradiction of sinners against himself, lest ye be wearied and faint in your minds.—HEBREWS 12:1–3

I didn't understand that the Christian journey with Jesus was a repeating cycle. It involves running, but running with *patience*. It involves the continual process of laying aside sin and weights—things that hinder our hearts for Him and slow our growth in grace. It involves the continual "resetting" of my focus upon Him and the ongoing *considering* of His suffering. Without this, as Scripture says, we will become *weary* and *faint*.

That's another way of saying, if you don't understand the renewing work—the daily grind of real Christianity—then you will become exhausted and empty.

When "Holiness" Becomes Unholy

In this faulty theology of my early spiritual growth I turned to rules and standards as my measuring stick of spiritual health—never mind love and relationship. My journey became a strict adherence to a code. Rather than using personal standards as simple, safe boundary lines of living, they became my personal measuring sticks of spiritual success. Keeping rules became my "definition of spiritual maturity." Spirituality became an exercise in *living under law* rather then *growing in grace*.

In Jesus' day, this was the very problem of the nation of Israel and the system of Judaism. It's why He rebuked the Pharisees—the best law-keepers of their day:

Woe unto you, scribes and Pharisees, hypocrites! for ye are like unto whited sepulchres, which indeed appear beautiful outward, but are within full of dead men's bones, and of all uncleanness.—MATTHEW 23:27

Ye hypocrites, well did Esaias prophesy of you, saying, This people draweth nigh unto me with their mouth, and honoureth me with their lips; but their heart is far from me. But in vain they do worship me, teaching for doctrines the commandments of men.—MATTHEW 15:7–9

Those who worked the hardest to discipline their behavior and keep their rules were the farthest from God in their hearts. Some of their laws were God-given. Some were man-made. Either way, the keeping of laws and standards became their god. They disciplined themselves, judged others, and measured spirituality by external indicators. They worshiped their own religiosity and good behavior. Jesus totally blew up their theological framework.

Like the Pharisees, rule-keeping became my goal and definition of spiritual success. My standards were high (as God deserves), and I scored myself pretty well. Unfortunately, I often measured myself and others by those "rules"—just like the Pharisees did. Even scarier, I was blind to it.

How is this wrong?

First, it minimizes God and the work of His Spirit. I tried to manufacture immediate goodness by appearance, rather than allowing God to produce genuine goodness over time—in myself and in others around me.

Second, it minimizes grace. It placed self-effort and personal discipline ahead of the spiritual and organic work of grace. It turned spirituality into something that could be manufactured and manipulated rather than cultivated and grown.

Third, it places my evaluation ahead of God's. I'm not my own judge. I'm not the judge of another. I'm a growing Christian being cultivated and nurtured forward by God. Trying to measure my growth or others' is a losing game. Who am I to evaluate others? Who am I to set the standard? Who am I to attempt to measure externally the spiritual maturity of others (James 4:12)?

Fourth, it is externally focused. Pharisees focused on behavior over heart. While I was focusing on the externals, I knew there was still pride, fear, anxiety, doubt, and distrust in my heart. My rules and standards served to "whitewash" the outside and compare well against others—but the inside was still a mess.

Fifth, it fosters compartmentalization and rationalization. The Pharisees rationalized their internal sins because they were externally good. They compartmentalized their spirituality. It's very easy to tolerate our own besetting sins, so long as we compensate with external success. We marginalize hidden sin and compartmentalize our Christian walk— not allowing the Holy Spirit to deal with our whole hearts. In this, we tend to minor on our areas of struggle, while majoring on our areas of strength. This is especially easy for pastors and ministry workers to do, because we magnify our "good works" to rationalize our need for repentance and renewal within.

Sixth, it removes the Holy Spirit's work in holy living. Self-generated holiness isn't holy. It might *appear* holy. The Pharisees *looked* holy. God is interested in generating true life-change by His power. When I focus on modifying and controlling my own behavior over loving and yielding to Jesus Christ, my flesh gets in the way of growth. It works for a while, but ultimately it's discouraging and prevents me from enjoying my relationship with Jesus.

Don't think I'm writing against personal standards or good behavior—I have personal and behavioral standards, and you will, too. But they should be the product of our "first love" of Jesus, not of our self-effort for Him. They should not define righteousness or maturity by human measurement. Don't fall into the trap of measuring yourself or others by externals. My *ability* to keep external rules is not necessarily a mark of depth or maturity.

Personal standards are simply boundaries to protect my life and testimony. They are not a box in which I try to place or measure every other Christian. I cannot be God. I cannot usurp the work of His Holy Spirit in others. It's an easy trap to fall into.

Real Holiness

As obedient children, not fashioning yourselves according to the former lusts in your ignorance: But as he which hath called you is holy, so be ye holy in all manner of conversation; Because it is written, Be ye holy; for I am holy.—1 Peter 1:14–16

The verses above clearly show us that God is absolutely interested in our holiness as His children—at every level. He calls us to grow in obedience (that's behavioral). He calls us to be transformed from our "former lusts" into His likeness (also behavioral). He desires for our "conversation"—our manner of life (again, behavioral)—to be holy. How so?

Holiness is simply another way of saying "righteousness" or "Christlikeness." Therefore, holiness plays out on the same three levels as our unfolding salvation.

Internal Holiness—You were declared holy through Jesus the moment you placed your faith in Him as Saviour. This is new birth. This is to be rescued from the *penalty* of sin.

External Holiness—You are being renewed and transformed in your mind and behavior, every day growing in grace, that your conversation (lifestyle) might be holy, even as your new nature is. Yielding to Jesus Christ will gradually transform your external life to be consistent with your new creature. This is the new mind. This is to be rescued from the *power* of sin.

Eternal Holiness—You will one day be redeemed, freed from flesh, to live forever in Heaven. This is the new body. This is to be rescued from the *presence* of sin.

Measuring Maturity

For we dare not make ourselves of the number, or compare ourselves with some that commend themselves: but they measuring themselves by themselves, and comparing themselves among themselves, are not wise.—2 CORINTHIANS 10:12

But God forbid that I should glory, save in the cross of our Lord Jesus Christ, by whom the world is crucified unto me, and I unto the world.
—GALATIANS 6:14

Who art thou that judgest another man's servant? to his own master he standeth or falleth. Yea, he shall be holden up: for God is able to make him stand.—ROMANS 14:4

There is one lawgiver, who is able to save and to destroy: who art thou that judgest another?—JAMES 4:12

Early Christians fell into the trap of external measurement and comparison. We do, too. We want to see visible success—in ourselves and others. We want to measure growth—somehow quantify success. Simply put, if you are still loving Jesus, walking with Him, and yielding to Him five or ten years from now—that is success! Faithfulness is success. Staying in the fight is success.

Rather than trying to measure my success by externals, God calls me to focus on the health of my heart and relationship with Him.

He's more interested in what He's doing *in* me than in what I'm doing *for* Him! The first takes care of the second. Obedience and honor to Jesus Christ will happen organically as I respond to His grace, rather than mechanically as a product of my self-effort. Anything I ever do *for* Him should always be an overflow of what He is first doing *in* me.

If I remain in love with Jesus, walking with Him, yielding to Him—the transforming work will continue. The great dangers in the Christian journey are *idolatry or defection*—lesser loves or giving up. These are the sins that most beset us.

> *Little children, keep yourselves from idols. Amen.*—1 JOHN 5:21

> *Keep yourselves in the love of God, looking for the mercy of our Lord Jesus Christ unto eternal life.*—JUDE 21

> *Take heed unto thyself, and unto the doctrine; continue in them: for in doing this thou shalt both save thyself, and them that hear thee.*—1 TIMOTHY 4:16

From the moment you were saved until you see Him, a fight for your heart—your first love—is in progress. There's a war raging over your *affections* and your *endurance*.

Quite often, you will feel that you are losing that war. The question of this chapter is, what do I do when I am? What happens when my love falters? What happens when I wander from Jesus or behave in a way that hinders my relationship with Him?

Jesus' Invitation to Fail Forward

For this we look back to what Jesus said to the church of Ephesus—a hardworking church that drifted off course in a subtle but critical way. Read carefully:

Unto the angel of the church of Ephesus write; These things saith he that holdeth the seven stars in his right hand, who walketh in the midst of the seven golden candlesticks; I know thy works, and thy labour, and thy patience, and how thou canst not bear them which are evil: and thou hast tried them which say they are apostles, and are not, and hast found them liars: And hast borne, and hast patience, and for my name's sake hast laboured, and hast not fainted. Nevertheless I have somewhat against thee, because thou hast left thy first love Remember therefore from whence thou art fallen, and repent, and do the first works; or else I will come unto thee quickly, and will remove thy candlestick out of his place, except thou repent.—REVELATION 2:1–5*

These Christians were behaving well by human standards, but were failing by God's standards. That's the problem with our attempts at measuring maturity—we don't have God's knowledge or eternal perspective, so our measurement is always inaccurate.

What did Jesus invite this church to do with their failure? Pay for it? Atone for it? Be punished for it? No. He invited them to remember and repent. He invited them to deal with their failure and return to their relationship with Him.

Remember where you came from. Real Christianity is a glorious struggle! It's a good fight of faith that involves failure and repentance.

Consider Joshua and the children of Israel. God promised that victory was theirs and the land would be won—but then God commanded them to *fight* for it. The fight involved some failure. The book of Joshua records several missteps—victory through failure, after failure, and in spite of failure.

Failure, and biblically dealing with failure, is a part of your Christian journey. So is victory! You will fail, and if you respond properly to your failure, you will continue fighting, in which case you will continue winning. Victory is sure—but only if you keep fighting! God brings victory in failure, through failure, after failure, and in spite of failure. What a marvelous Saviour! (See Luke 21:31–32.)

The only way Joshua and his armies could lose the fight was if they quit fighting. Failure was never final, unless they decided to quit. Failure was merely a temporary setback that called forth remembrance, repentance, and restoration.

So it is with your walk with Jesus. Struggle means failure. But this chapter is about how you respond to failure.

When the Christians at Ephesus failed, Jesus said, *"Remember therefore from whence thou art fallen."* You may have "fallen" but you haven't fallen so far as your "pre-salvation" state. Remember the love that called you to Jesus. Remember the love that you once had for Him. Remember when it was about *relationship*, not *religion—loving* more than *doing*.

Remember God ordained this struggle. God allowed it. Your old nature died an immediate death. Your flesh dies a slow death. You are engaged in an epic struggle where your daily *faith* glorifies God, even though you fail. The faith you express when you repent, get back up, and fight forward is faith that brings God glory and pleasure!

> *Finally, my brethren, be strong in the Lord, and in the power of his might. Put on the whole armour of God, that ye may be able to stand against the wiles of the devil. For we wrestle not against flesh and blood, but against principalities, against powers, against the rulers of the darkness of this world, against spiritual wickedness in high places.*
> —EPHESIANS 6:10–12

Remember that there is no condemnation. Jesus was condemned for you. He paid it all on the cross. There is simply nothing left for which you could be condemned. The cross was completely sufficient. The cross satisfied all of God's righteous demands for your sin. When your heart condemns you, remember that's just flesh! Don't buy the lie. Don't listen to the flesh. His Spirit will remind you—"No condemnation!"

> *There is therefore now no condemnation to them which are in Christ Jesus, who walk not after the flesh, but after the Spirit.*—ROMANS 8:1

> *For if our heart condemn us, God is greater than our heart, and knoweth all things.*—1 JOHN 3:20

It's important to note that Holy Spirit *conviction* is not the same as *condemnation*. God's Spirit will *convict* you of sin and wrong. He will call you back to Himself, but He will not *condemn* you. Self-condemnation is always *destructive*. Spirit-conviction is always *restorative*.

Remember that this struggle serves a purpose. The winning of this daily war is not a "try harder" thing. It's a "trust deeper" or "yield greater" thing. You don't win by setting up rules or restrictions or by renewing self-effort. You win by repenting and returning to "first love."

The winning of this war is found in humbling myself, by faith, and trusting His grace, moment by moment. It's living dependently every day in the same gospel of grace that saved you.

The cross of Jesus isn't merely a ticket out of eternal judgment. The cross is your covering every day. The gospel is not only applicable the moment you were saved. It's applicable every moment after. Real Christianity is total immersion into the gospel. To be saved is to be completely engulfed in grace and unconditional love and completely dependent upon God's Spirit within for the rest of your life.

Living in Jesus involves preaching the gospel to yourself every single day, reminding yourself that you are accepted by His grace and then letting that grace motivate and empower you to express His nature and grow into His image.

Real Christians and Repentance

When you were a child, what did you do when you broke your parents' or teacher's rules? You probably tried to hide it, rationalize it, deny it, lie about it, or blame someone else for it.

Think about those responses—*hide, rationalize, deny, lie, blame.* They all have some things in common.

First, they are all about avoiding punishment. Nobody likes to be "in trouble." Children hate being "in trouble" and the punishment that follows, so they all play the game of avoiding "being caught."

Second, they are all destructive to growth. A child that hides, rationalizes, denies, lies, or blames is avoiding more than trouble. He's avoiding growing in character. In fact, he's fueling bad character. Hiding failure always prevents growth.

Third, they are all destructive to relationships. A child that is hiding or deceiving authority, is also damaging the relationship. Deception destroys closeness.

Here's the point. God has gone to extreme measures to deal so effectively and finally with your failure, that there's only one thing left to do when you fail—acknowledge it and run to Him. You can't pay for it—He did. You can't hide it—He already knows about it. You can't run from Him or avoid Him—He's everywhere. You can't earn your way back—He's already done that for you.

You have nothing to gain by the silly behaviors you learned as a child. God doesn't fall for hiding, rationalizing, denying, lying, or blame-shifting. And because of grace, there's no point whatsoever in doing those things when you fail. The only thing left is to acknowledge the sin and turn back to Him seeking His grace and help!

This is exactly where He wants you to be regularly! It's called *repentance.*

As a Christian, you're prone to wander. Will your failure be final? Or like Joshua, will you continue to fight? Will you fall away from Jesus, or will you answer His call to remember and repent? Will you stay on the boat, or, like Peter, will you swim as fast as you can to Jesus?

Repentance is a change of thinking. It's acknowledging sin and running to Jesus. And as His child, I can always run to Him! His arms are always open.

Jesus is someone to run to, not from! He's someone to hide in, not from!

My gut response to failure is to run *from* Jesus, but He calls me to run *to* Him. As a kid, I ran from my failure. I hid my disobedience. I ran from being punished. I did everything I could to keep my parents from "catching me." In Jesus, there's no need for that. He offers restoration, grace, and help. Why would I run from Him?

The only compulsion to run *from* Jesus would be that I've allowed my heart to love sin more than love Him.

Do you get it? God never wants you to worry about your stability or security with Him. He never wants you to assume a hiding, running, blaming, or denying posture. He desires for you to be absolutely comfortable coming completely clean with Him, in total transparency and confession. He already knows the truth; He already paid for the failure. He has removed every obstacle to closeness with Him, except your will.

The church at Ephesus was failing in their first love. Their love of working *for* Jesus overshadowed their love *of* Jesus. So Jesus called them, not to restitution or recompense, but to *repentance*. He didn't ask them to pay for their crimes through penance. He invited them to return to their first love. And so it is with me and you.

If you're going to survive and enjoy the Christian journey, you'll have to become really good at regularly repenting. Why? Because every faithful

Christian is a struggling Christian. Every successful Christian is a regularly failing Christian who continually "gets back up" through repentance.

Let's press on and discover what it means to accept Jesus' invitation to be a "comeback kid!"

Twelve

Comeback Kids
Getting a Biblical Grasp on Repentance

Do you remember learning to ride a bike? If you succeeded, it was only because you kept getting back on the bike after you fell off. You learned how to come back after a fall! I still bear some scars on my knees from my "bike-learning" experiences. Fortunately, getting back on the bike was easy. I was a comeback kid. In fact, I still am, spiritually. You can be, too!

With Jesus, getting back into fellowship with Him is *always* an option—ALWAYS! And it's "easy." That doesn't mean it was easy for Him. It doesn't mean it's cheap. It means He's paid all the price, and returning to Him is as simple for you as it was for the prodigal son. That's what inexhaustible grace is. Returning to Him in repentance is always an open door.

Here's the big idea: *Real Christians are repeat offenders but regular repenters.*

Joyful Christians learn how to turn back quickly and often, every time they fail. They are quick to humble themselves and acknowledge or "confess" their sins—not to a priest or pastor—but to Jesus. They deal honestly with their failure.

They see Jesus as someone to run *to* not *from*. They know He is someone to hide *in* not *from!* Jesus is not on a warpath for you, He's on a *rescue mission* for you!

Unfortunately, there's a lot of confusion about repentance and what it is. Let's explore what it isn't.

It is not guilt, shame, or condemnation. If you're experiencing this, it's not God, it's your accuser or yourself. Conviction always calls you to Jesus; condemnation pushes you away from Him.

It is not merely regret, remorse, or self-abasement. While you may regret or sorrow over your failure, God isn't merely looking for a sad emotion. He's looking for a humble heart—a tender heart that will resume a yielded posture before Him. Jesus took all of your beating—there's no value in beating yourself up, ever!

It is not penance, atonement, payment, or punishment. There's nothing left to pay—Jesus paid it all!

It's not asking forgiveness over and over again. Jesus is propitiation. This word means the full payment for sin that allows God to forever stand in your favor, on your side, with open arms of grace, no matter what. He's already forgiven you.

It isn't regaining or reclaiming salvation. Once reborn, you can never become unborn. Nothing can separate you from God's love as your Father. Repentance isn't about becoming saved again. You are only saved once. But you can restore your relational closeness with Jesus over and over again.

What Is Repentance?

As many as I love, I rebuke and chasten: be zealous therefore, and repent.—REVELATION 3:19

For a just man falleth seven times, and riseth up again: but the wicked shall fall into mischief.—PROVERBS 24:16

The word *zealous* means "to be moved with energetic or earnest desire"—in other words, "RUN TO JESUS!"

Repentance literally means "to think differently." It's an acknowledging of wrong thinking and living, and an acceptance of the mind of Christ—a renewed mind. It's an acknowledgement of the truth. It is the discovery or submission to truth that leads to change. It is selecting a different option, taking a divergent path—turning from sin and to Jesus.

In meekness instructing those that oppose themselves; if God peradventure will give them repentance to the acknowledging of the truth;—2 TIMOTHY 2:25

For those who don't know Jesus as your personal Saviour, it's the decision to own your sin, your violation of God's laws, and your need of justification and salvation from Christ alone. Salvation is repentance.

For those who know Jesus as Saviour, repentance is a recurring habit of real Christian living. It's the art of listening to the Holy Spirit, agreeing with Him, and allowing Him to change your thinking and living.

Repentance is a willing, personal acknowledgement of sin and renewed yielding to Jesus for grace-driven life change.

God doesn't ask you to pay for your sin, to make up for it, to atone for it, or to just feel badly about it—He calls you to acknowledge it, confess it, and forsake it. He calls you to run from sin and to Him. Let's break this definition down.

Acknowledge it. Agree with God that it is sinful, hurtful, destructive.

Confess it. Admit to it before God. No hiding. No rationalizing. No blaming. No excusing. No tolerating. No justifying. No ignoring.

Forsake it. Make a choice of will (in Christ) to be dead to it, and to serve righteousness.

Remember, this is a habit of healthy Christianity. Real Christians do this over and over again, reflexively—thousands of times in their long journey with Jesus. You can never exhaust God's invitation to repent and return to Him.

Repentance is the act of taking responsibility for my sin—removing the games we play with God and getting real before Him. It brings us to a place where our relationship with God can be whole and healthy. Closeness and real change is made possible when we genuinely respond to our sin with a repentant heart.

This is critical—repentance itself doesn't generate life change, but it does bring me to a place where life change is possible by the Holy Spirit.

Where repentance gets muddy or confusing is when we try to evaluate or measure its authenticity. Some turn repentance into a "work" necessary for salvation or a "work" necessary for recovery with God. In other words, I must have a certain, *measurable level* of remorse, regret, or intent for my repentance to be genuine. That's *penance*, not repentance.

Repentance is changing my mind and agreeing with God.

As a father, I've had the painful delight of debating with three growing children for hundreds of hours over the past twenty-two years. As I was with my parents, my children have often been stubborn, hard-headed, and standing in staunch disagreement with me. Their sin was blatantly clear to me, but to them, it was easily justified, rationalized, or blame-shifted. So, a discussion ensued. A process of breaking down their hardness unfolded.

On some occasions, perhaps when the facts were unclear or when I jumped to a conclusion, I was wrong and needed to repent—to acknowledge truth and change my mind. In most instances, my children were wrong and needed to repent and grow.

Do you know the greatest obstacles to their growth? Pride. Justification. Blame-shifting. Lying. Rationalizing. Their *argumentative posture* was non-repentance. It was a wall preventing growth and fatherly nurture. I couldn't help a hard heart that refused help. God often referred to Israel as a "stiff-necked people." "*But they obeyed not, neither inclined their ear, but made their neck stiff, that they might not hear, nor receive instruction*" (Jeremiah 17:23). Notice, their unrepentant posture would not hear or receive instruction.

So with my children, growth was only possible when they softened their hearts and repented—changed their minds. Repentance wasn't about tears of remorse or hitting a "ten" on the Richter scale of grief. Sometimes that happened; sometimes it didn't. In most cases, their emotions were peripheral to the repentance process. Their hardness of heart and stubbornness of mind is what needed to change. They were opposing themselves and needed me to instruct them with a spirit of meekness in hopes that God would bring them to a point of repentance and acknowledging truth (2 Timothy 2:25).

After hours of loving and firm instruction (lecturing, if you ask them), a "breakthrough" would happen. The light would finally come on in the heart. They would finally get it. God would soften the spirit, the child would acknowledge the truth, and closeness or growth would resume. The stubborn posture toward me changed—from hardness and resistance to *tenderness* and *teachability*. They moved from *rejection* to *reception* of truth.

This is a beautiful picture of repentance. This spiritual, intellectual, and relational softening and breakthrough is what real repentance produces.

How often as a Christian I have found myself playing the hard-hearted child. I have loved my sin and my self-will. God's Spirit attempts to convict, but I push back. I refuse to return. Sin is pleasurable for a season. Selfishness is seductive. The flesh doesn't die easily. I argue with God, justify myself, and willfully deny what His Spirit is trying to teach me.

In God's gracious longsuffering, He patiently deals with me—teaching, convicting, chastening—calling my heart to soften before Him. The longer I resist, the more I struggle and grow cold towards His love. The sooner I soften, the better my whole life.

At some point, I break. My heart softens, my will dies, and my spirit turns back to Jesus. Repentance causes me to acknowledge that He is right and I am wrong.

Repentance is when the light of truth comes on in your heart. You see sin as it is, God as He is, grace as it is, and you RUN to JESUS, acknowledging truth. Your heart softens toward Him and His Word, your mind embraces truth, and once again your spiritual growth in Jesus resumes.

This is why repentance is a wonderful thing. It is a spiritual breakthrough that allows God's grace to powerfully and wonderfully work in your heart.

Repentance is a change of mind that allows God to produce a change of heart!

What Leads to Repentance?

You might think that pain or punishment is what leads us to repentance. In other words, when God brings the hammer down, we will finally give in to His "wrath" and turn to Him. Threat of punishment may lead to surface repentance, but this is not the heart-changing repentance that God desires for His children. As a child of God the "punishment" concept is a distorted view of God. If God were this way, it would only mean that Jesus wasn't the propitiation—the full satisfaction of God's righteous demands. Jesus took all of our punishment (or penalty) on the cross.

> And he is the propitiation for our sins: and not for ours only, but also for the sins of the whole world.—1 JOHN 2:2

> Herein is love, not that we loved God, but that he loved us, and sent his Son to be the propitiation for our sins.—1 JOHN 4:10

Sin may have consequences. You may endure chastening. But these things are never punitive. So God is never saying to you, His child, "Repent or be punished."

So if punishment shouldn't motivate repentance, what should? Enter the wonderful gospel—the grace of God is the greatest motivator of repentance. See it for yourself:

> Or despisest thou the riches of his goodness and forbearance and longsuffering; not knowing that the goodness of God leadeth thee to repentance?—ROMANS 2:4

What motivates me to repent? Not pain. Not problems. Not threat.

Goodness. God's amazing goodness leads to repentance! How in the world is that possible?

We are programmed to believe that only threat (negative consequences) would motivate repentance. It does, but not always *genuine* repentance. Threat-motivated repentance is often forced or contrived— it is motivated by self-interest and self-protection. God doesn't desire forced repentance. He desires your willful return and receptivity.

He desires for you to see Him as better than your sin.

Therefore, His limitless goodness is what most genuinely motivates us to joyfully choose Him over sin.

In Luke 15, Jesus told a story about a son who rebelled against his father. He took his inheritance, left home, and wasted his substance on "riotous living." It wasn't long before the rebel was living in poverty, feeding pigs, and regretting his decisions. The beauty of the story is that he decided to return home. He repented. He decided to go home and do penance before his father—asking to be a slave rather than a son.

Imagine his amazement and surprise when his father would not even give him the chance to do penance! What he *expected* was nothing like what he *experienced*.

He had no clue his father was waiting with eager anticipation. He had no idea he simply needed to change his mind and return to open arms. He mistook repentance and presumed penance was in order.

How surprised he must have been to find his father watching and waiting, then running and embracing! How delighted he must have been to run into those open arms and find unconditional love and inexhaustible grace. How much brokenness and destitution must have instantly flooded away in the love of that embrace. How awesome that moment must have been—to experience immediate and absolute closeness, love, and security with his father.

I'll bet he was glad he ran *to* his father rather than *from* his father. I would guess at some point he thought, *I should have done this a long time ago!*

How much sooner would the prodigal son have returned to his father, if he knew his father's heart? One thing is sure—he would have eaten fewer corn husks and spent fewer nights in brokenness and poverty.

This is a picture of repentance. You are the prodigal son. Jesus is the loving Father—waiting with eager anticipation. If you knew His goodness—if you knew His love and grace—you would run to Him! This is how the "goodness of God leadeth thee to repentance." His goodness opens the door wide. His grace removes all threat and all reason to stay away.

You can stay in the pigpen of sin, but God's goodness is far better, and the way home has already been provided!

What Hinders Repentance?

There are a few things that will keep you from repenting as you should:

Love for sin—When we love sin more than we love Jesus, we refuse to repent. There are only two motivations for repentance and obedience to God—love or law (have to or want to). Law always leads me to more failure and discouragement. Law always breaks down. The only sustainable motivation for repentance and obedience to God is love.

Pride or self-will—A stubborn heart remains trapped in idolatry, and God will persistently chasten to deliver me from this self-destructive posture. Just ask Jonah.

So often we think of the "great fish" as Jonah's punishment, and we couldn't be more wrong. The fish that swallowed Jonah was the grace of God. Jonah was destroying himself. He was stubbornly running from God, refusing to repent, to the point that he said, "Throw me overboard." He was suicidal. So God, in His grace and goodness, sent a great fish to save Jonah from himself and lead him to repentance.

Ignorance of God's goodness—Sin is always *hurtful,* and God's commands are always *helpful.* He is a Father, and He always has your best interest at heart. Sin is a destroyer and always leads you toward destruction. Repentance is believing and running to Him.

For this is the love of God, that we keep his commandments: and his commandments are not grievous.—1 JOHN 5:3

Sin's pleasure—Sin just hasn't hurt me enough to break my idolatry and bring me to repentance. With this mindset, I haven't hit rock bottom yet. There are two times we repent—when we love Jesus enough, or when sin becomes painful enough.

Why Is Repentance Repetitive?

The Apostle John was one of Jesus' closest friends and followers. He was a young man whose life was radically changed by Jesus. He loved Jesus deeply. As an old man, after a lifetime of following Jesus, John wrote these words to real, first-century Christians:

My little children, these things write I unto you, that ye sin not. And if any man sin, we have an advocate with the Father, Jesus Christ the righteous: And he is the propitiation for our sins: and not for ours only, but also for the sins of the whole world.—1 JOHN 2:1–2

He begins by saying, "I'm writing all of this so that you won't sin." Make no mistake, God is transforming your behavior. As you authentically grow in His grace, you will sin less. Sin's strongholds in your life will weaken and loosen over your lifelong journey with Jesus. It will probably not happen as fast as you hope, but it will happen.

But then John immediately says, "But when you sin, you have an advocate in Jesus Christ." An advocate is a defender. In other words, when you sin—RUN TO JESUS! He's your justifier, your savior, your redeemer—not just one time when you were saved, but every day as you fail and get back up—He always stands in your defense, on your side, in your corner.

In this we understand that real daily victory will be something less than ultimate and final. In our daily growth, there will be some succeeding, some failing, some repenting, and some getting back up—it's a process of failing forward in grace.

What does this teach us about victory?

First, victory will be incremental. Some days you will feel like you gained ground. Other days you will feel like you lost ground. Most days, you'll wonder whether you gained or lost. Often victory is so incremental that it's imperceptible. Don't be discouraged. This is real Christianity.

But grow in grace, and in the knowledge of our Lord and Saviour Jesus Christ. To him be glory both now and for ever. Amen.—2 PETER 3:18

Victory will be seasonal. God knows what He's doing in your life. There's a lot of growth ahead, which means there's a lot of sanctifying work that is still to be done. Maybe you desire victory in one area while He's growing you in another. God is the builder, you're the project. He's the potter, you're the clay. Don't question what's He's doing. Just sit still and stay soft.

Being confident of this very thing, that he which hath begun a good work in you will perform it until the day of Jesus Christ:—PHILIPPIANS 1:6

Victory will not always be measurable. Your estimation or measurement of yourself or others is always inaccurate. You don't have enough information with which to make an error-free measurement of God's work. We're not to measure ourselves or others. We're to keep our eyes on Jesus and keep pressing forward for Him.

Looking unto Jesus the author and finisher of our faith; who for the joy that was set before him endured the cross, despising the shame, and is set down at the right hand of the throne of God.—HEBREWS 12:2

Victory will one day be final. Bank on it! This war is already won—no matter how you feel. At a daily, microscopic level, you'll win some battles and lose some battles. At a cosmic, macroscopic level—the war is won and Jesus is King. You're on the winning side. Hold on!

But thanks be to God, which giveth us the victory through our Lord Jesus Christ.—1 CORINTHIANS 15:57

Incremental, seasonal, immeasurable victory makes repentance a wonderful, amazing, welcoming gift! Get good at it. It's the act of running back to Jesus' loving, open arms every time you find yourself distant or struggling. He has gone to extreme measures to make repentance possible.

Good news, real Christian, you are never more than one step of repentance away from God.

Real Christians are comeback kids! They are repeat offenders but regular repenters.

Run to Him!

Now I rejoice, not that ye were made sorry, but that ye sorrowed to repentance....—2 CORINTHIANS 7:9

Thirteen

Growth Points
How Faith in Jesus Grows Greater

Gardening has never been my thing. Many of my friends are proficient at growing good fruit, but when it comes to plant life, my only gift is *killing* it. Give me a plant and you're pretty much sending it to death row. I'm a horticultural death sentence.

It's sad, really. It's not that I don't like fruit or vegetables; I'm just not patient enough. If I buy a strawberry bush, I want that thing to produce big, lush strawberries within a few days—*hours* would even be better. I want a strawberry machine! Plug it in, turn it on, and watch the strawberries pop out.

The one time I actually bought and planted strawberry bushes, I kept them alive just long enough to grow strawberries for all the rodents and birds to eat. I'm not sure what I expected—maybe that the berries would protect, cultivate, and harvest themselves—from my backyard to my shortcake in short order and minimal effort. I was a disastrous strawberry farmer. Four bushes, three months of neglect, and every berry went to the mice and birds.

Cultivating fruit requires patience, protection, and persistence—it requires attention and intention. As for me, why get dirty, wait for weeks (or months), fight off every kind of insect and animal, and toil in all kinds of weather—when I can drive a mile, hand over a debit card, and walk out of a grocery store with fresh fruit right now! No sweat. No toil. No effort. No sacrifice. Just fruit—right now! That's what I'm talking about.

Isn't that what we want in the Christian life? We want the fruit of the Spirit immediately, with minimal effort, no struggle, no hassle, no wait. We treat our Christian life like a steroid boost that should help us be "super-human" at this thing called life. Our combined impatience and eagerness expects significant forward momentum and spiritual fruitfulness, in abundance, as soon as possible.

Hopefully, by now you're understanding this isn't the way God designed real Christianity. A relationship with Jesus produces wonderful fruit, but only over a long time, with great patience, plenty of personal attention, and serious cultivation. Real Christianity is a marathon, not a sprint. It's a relationship, not a machine.

The central message of this chapter is simply this: *Faith grows with intention and attention.*

As God works in you, He desires to cultivate fruit from your life. This fruit is *His* product—*His* workmanship. It is all His doing, but it's going to result in your visible transformation and service. It's going to bring forth behaviors, labor, and works that magnify Jesus and further His gospel.

The cultivation of your faith, like a garden, will bring forth something evident, tangible, and real in the way of Christlike attitudes, behaviors, and lifestyles. You will *desire* to obey, and you *will* obey—not because you *have to*, but because you *want to*. Growing in grace and walking with Jesus will produce new desires and new doings. Your values will change. Your behaviors will change.

In other words, your faith is not merely an intangible, internal work. Faith isn't invisible or inactive. Biblical faith is always effectual and active—it produces visible transformation and obedience to Jesus. Belief produces behavior. What you believe will change how you behave.

> *Yea, a man may say, Thou hast faith, and I have works: shew me thy*
> *faith without thy works, and I will shew thee my faith by my works.*
> —JAMES 2:18

Finally Ready for God's Work

Consider Peter again. Before his brokenness and failure at the crucifixion, Peter wasn't ready for the real work God desired to do through Him. Peter needed to become intimately acquainted with his utter weakness. At that point, he would either quit (which he did) or he would humble himself and run back in total dependence upon Jesus. That humility mixed with faith would allow Jesus to do His work in and through Peter.

Shortly after the reclaiming of Peter in John 21, Peter stands in grace and God's power and declares the gospel in Jerusalem at the feast of Pentecost. On this occasion, over three thousand people believed and were baptized. Amazing fruit was the product of absolute humiliation and active dependence upon Jesus. Peter was not the performer of the work, the Holy Spirit was—Peter was just the conduit, and he knew it. Pentecost could not happen prior to brokenness.

Early in the book of John, the disciples asked Jesus an important question, and He gave them a seemingly strange answer.

> *Then said they unto him, What shall we do, that we might work the*
> *works of God? Jesus answered and said unto them, This is the work of*
> *God, that ye believe on him whom he hath sent.*—JOHN 6:28–29

The disciples wanted to do God's work, but Jesus clearly says, "God's work is to believe on Me!" Strange? Seems so, but not really. The beginning of all good works of God is utter dependence upon Him—faith.

Created unto Good Works

If you have been wondering "What's my role in this? Where does my effort come in?" This is it. God's Word has a lot to say about the good works to which God has called you. His work in you is designed to cultivate fruit— good works flowing *from* you.

His grace is meant not only to flow *to* you but *through* you!

Scripture is clear that God calls you to a holy life as well as a fruitful life. He calls you to good works—not *for* salvation but as a *product of* salvation. The natural result of genuine faith is an increasingly "like-Jesus" lifestyle. The outgrowth of yielding to God's Spirit is growth in good works that glorify God.

The works don't *earn* salvation or favor. They don't *keep* you in God's grace or earn merit with Him. But they do glorify, honor, and please Him. A lifestyle that expresses your faith and exalts your Saviour is well-pleasing to God. The more you understand grace, the more you will be motivated to yield to Jesus and let Him live His life through you.

Take a look at the many ways God says that His grace will become *visible* in a growing lifestyle of *good works* and *godly fruit*:

> *But the fruit of the Spirit is love, joy, peace, longsuffering, gentleness,*
> *goodness, faith, Meekness, temperance: against such there is no law.*
> —GALATIANS 5:22–23

For we are his workmanship, created in Christ Jesus unto good works, which God hath before ordained that we should walk in them. —EPHESIANS 2:10

And this I pray, that your love may abound yet more and more in knowledge and in all judgment; Being filled with the fruits of righteousness, which are by Jesus Christ, unto the glory and praise of God.—PHILIPPIANS 1:9, 11

Remembering without ceasing your work of faith, and labour of love, and patience of hope in our Lord Jesus Christ, in the sight of God and our Father;—1 THESSALONIANS 1:3

And the Lord make you to increase and abound in love one toward another, and toward all men, even as we do toward you: —1 THESSALONIANS 3:12

All scripture is given by inspiration of God, and is profitable for doctrine, for reproof, for correction, for instruction in righteousness: That the man of God may be perfect, throughly furnished unto all good works. —2 TIMOTHY 3:16–17

In all things shewing thyself a pattern of good works: in doctrine shewing uncorruptness, gravity, sincerity,—TITUS 2:7

And let us consider one another to provoke unto love and to good works:—HEBREWS 10:24

Yea, a man may say, Thou hast faith, and I have works: shew me thy faith without thy works, and I will shew thee my faith by my works. —JAMES 2:18

My little children, let us not love in word, neither in tongue; but in deed and in truth.—1 JOHN 3:18

All of these verses indicate that a growing faith takes time and attention. Like a garden, your faith must be cultivated. You cannot *produce* growth, but you can nurture your faith in a healthy environment where growth will happen. You cannot *manufacture* fruit, but you can *cultivate* health that leads to fruit.

In other words, growth is a product of *right conditions*. You can't force self-effort that matures you spiritually, but you can immerse your faith into an environment that is conducive to growth. Healthy conditions will nurture a growing faith and a fruitful life.

Intention and Attention

Staying in love and staying close to my wife is not something that happens by accident. It happens by intent and it requires time and attention. We plan it. We decide to be close. We determine to spend time together. We intentionally cultivate, resolve, converse, and commune. We protect our relationship with boundaries that keep us from drifting apart. We deliberately plan to focus on each other. We premeditate special times for each other.

As I write these words I've just come past another birthday, and my wife and family were incredibly kind and thoughtful to make it memorable and meaningful. Dana made a special trip to the grocery store in the snow! She bought my favorite foods. She chose and wrapped gifts. She penned a wonderful, thoughtful message of love. She gave a lot of *intention* and *attention* to cultivating and expressing her love for me.

If you stopped her and asked, "Why are you doing this?" She would not have said, "Because I have to." "Because he will get angry if I don't." "Because I don't want him to leave me." "Because I want him to like me."

She would have simply said, *"Because I love him."*

Her love compels her to *express love*. She's not afraid of me. She's not motivated by anything less than love. Your faith relationship with Jesus should also be motivated by love.

Your relationship will be close and abundant only as you give it intention and attention. It will be genuine and real as you are motivated by love. It will produce good works that glorify and magnify Him, only as you are motivated by love. It will be organic, natural, authentic. Your good works will not be forced or driven. Living a godly life will not be a *burden* but a *delight*. Growing to be more like Jesus will be a natural overflow of a love relationship, not an artificial show for a distant deity.

If you ever get to the point where you are "doing" the Christian life because you "have to," something is terribly wrong. As in Isaiah's day, God would say to you as He did His people, "Put away all of your 'good works' and 'religious traditions'—your heart is far from Me!"

As we've seen, the Christian life becomes terribly frustrating and disappointing, redundantly systematic and even empty when we present God with obedience and worship that doesn't flow from faith and love.

A healthy love relationship requires strategic cultivation. Like a garden or a fruit tree, your faith can be alive and healthy, or it can be dry and distant. The state of your faith will depend upon the intention and attention you give it.

So the question is, what are healthy conditions for faith? What can I do to cultivate growth? What can I do in the way of *attention* and *intention* that will grow my faith?

If you could travel the world and interview thousands of mature and healthy Christians, you would come up with some basic things that will keep your faith healthy. God uses these things over and over to cultivate your spiritual health and growth. If you will commit and keep coming back to these things, your faith will grow strong, your roots will grow deep, and your life will become fruitful by God's work in you.

Here they are:

Growth Point 1—Communication from the Word

So then faith cometh by hearing, and hearing by the word of God. —ROMANS 10:17

For this cause also thank we God without ceasing, because, when ye received the word of God which ye heard of us, ye received it not as the word of men, but as it is in truth, the word of God, which effectually worketh also in you that believe.—1 THESSALONIANS 2:13

As newborn babes, desire the sincere milk of the word, that ye may grow thereby:—1 PETER 2:2

God has ordained that the first and most effective method of growing faith is to receive the communicated Word of God. God's Word is alive with infinite truth, and hearing it well taught will make it come alive to you. Hearing the truth will change your life as nothing else.

Do everything you can to fill your life with the received Word. This will most likely begin with a Bible-believing pastor and a healthy church family where you can regularly hear God's Word presented with doctrinal purity and practical clarity. Without this, your faith will not be healthy or fruitful.

Growth Point 2—Community with Believers

And they continued stedfastly in the apostles' doctrine and fellowship, and in breaking of bread, and in prayers.—ACTS 2:42

Not forsaking the assembling of ourselves together, as the manner of some is; but exhorting one another: and so much the more, as ye see the day approaching.—HEBREWS 10:25

Wherefore comfort yourselves together, and edify one another, even as also ye do.—1 THESSALONIANS 5:11

But exhort one another daily, while it is called To day; lest any of you be hardened through the deceitfulness of sin.—HEBREWS 3:13

God's greatest greenhouse for growing faith is the local church.

Early Christians were interdependent—together dependent upon Jesus. They committed themselves to community—doing faith together. Jesus gave His life for this concept. It's called *church,* and it's vital that you become a part of a healthy, Bible-believing, local church where God can use relationships and community to strengthen your faith.

Real Christianity is not a solo journey. God designed us to *need* each other. He calls us together—to encourage, to worship, to edify each other, to pray for one another. You can't do this alone.

Every time you find a Christian growing in maturity, you will find other believers whom God used to strengthen that Christian. You will find a church family supporting, praying, and cheering each other on. You will find healthy believers assembling, comforting, and serving. This is healthy Christianity and healthy church life.

Much of the New Testament is given to describing this church life and how to protect it. Jesus cares passionately about His people gathering together in grace. Love among believers is so important to Jesus that He said it's the one thing that will cause the world to believe the gospel!

By this shall all men know that ye are my disciples, if ye have love one to another.—JOHN 13:35

Satan tries to divide and isolate Christians. If he can keep you from church, from gathering with other believers, he can keep your faith weak and anemic. If you want a growing faith, immerse yourself into a biblical church and develop strong community with believers.

One more thought on this—always remember a healthy church is about sharing community in Jesus Christ. It's a body of believers growing in faith together. It's about *relationships* before *activity*. And ultimately it's about using those relationships to magnify Jesus and witness of Him to those who don't know Him.

Growth Point 3—Communion with Jesus

But his delight is in the law of the LORD; and in his law doth he meditate day and night. And he shall be like a tree planted by the rivers of water, that bringeth forth his fruit in his season; his leaf also shall not wither; and whatsoever he doeth shall prosper.—PSALM 1:2–3

Behold, I stand at the door, and knock: if any man hear my voice, and open the door, I will come in to him, and will sup with him, and he with me.—REVELATION 3:20

The first two growth points are about *external* support for your faith. At some point, cultivating your own faith becomes personal.

All three of my children, when born, required constant attention. Their health and safety was completely a product of *external care.* We fed them, changed them, dressed them, and nurtured them. But eventually, they grew, and today they care for themselves.

Do they still need parents and family? Yes. But at the same time, their care is not singularly dependent upon others. Similarly, your faith, when young, is dependent upon the communicated Word and community with believers. You'll never outgrow this, but personally communing with Jesus is the next step. Your own personal, daily walk with Jesus is vital for a growing and fruitful faith.

This is one-on-one time between you and Jesus. This is you opening up your heart, talking with Him, and letting His Word talk to you. Nothing else can take the place of this intimate time between you and God—and nothing can do for your heart what time with God can!

As Jesus Himself withdrew to spend time alone with His Father, so He desires to commune in relationship with you. It is easy to neglect this, but your relationship will grow distant and your Christian journey will become boring and routine. Staying close to Jesus is a personal choice. Cultivating your heart of love for Him is a daily and weekly process.

Whatever you do, don't turn this into a "have to." Keep it in the "want to" category. Read His Word, talk to Him, keep your walk with Him fresh and alive. Don't get stuck in systematic ruts. Your relationship with Jesus is not a scientific system. It's a dynamic, organic relationship. You can't make it a machine, but if you do, you will lose that first love.

Growth Point 4—Cataclysmic Events

And we know that all things work together for good to them that love God, to them who are the called according to his purpose.—ROMANS 8:28

One of the great doctrines of the Christian faith is the sovereignty of God—the truth that God is absolutely in control of all events in time and eternity. For you, this means that nothing enters your life without an eternal purpose and significance. Every hardship or trial will serve some growing and glorifying purpose of God.

Real Christianity isn't a *problem-free* life—it's a *promise-filled* life.

You will have problems and hardships, but now that you have a relationship with Jesus, you will no longer face those problems alone. You have His presence to comfort, His truth to guide, His promises to claim, and His wisdom to see the bigger picture.

Every healthy Christian can point to a time in his life when events and circumstances went crazy, but God proved Himself to be a present help and reality. For me it was cancer. Every mature Christian has stories of impossible circumstances and how God came through, answered prayer, or led him through by His strength and grace.

The question is, will you allow cataclysmic events to *flatten* you or *fortify* you? Will you see the events in your life through the eyes of faith or eyes of distress? Every cataclysmic event can become a catalyst for growth. Every hardship can be a time when you grow closer to Jesus.

Just remember, the prelude to seeing God come through is an alarming event that causes you to wonder where He is!

When you face calamity, consider this—*my circumstances are no mistake!* They are carefully designed and allowed by God to bring about growth and maturity in my life.

Our typical response to trouble is, *"God, get me out!"* A growing faith would look through a different lens and pray, *"God, grow me through!"*

The next time you face cataclysmic events, start praying, "God, what are You teaching me through these circumstances? Please help me see Your hand at work in my life."

Shortly after my cancer diagnosis, I was at a preaching engagement, and I had the opportunity to visit with my uncle and aunt who lived nearby. Up to that point I was having a hard time seeing anything but the "bad news" of cancer. On the outside, I was saying the right things, but inside, my heart was still having a pity party.

I'll never forget sitting down to dinner that night. As we joined hands, my uncle prayed over the meal. He paused and very gently and deliberately said these words:

"Lord Jesus, we thank You for the work that You are doing in Cary's body right now...."

I don't remember anything else he prayed that night, but I will never forget those words. I immediately fought back the tears of relief as the realization hit me. God, very poignantly, said to my spirit, "This is *My* work—trust Me." Wow! I hadn't viewed cancer as a "work He was doing in me" until that moment.

Now, nearly three years later, I can say with absolute certainty, those words were true, then and now.

In the most cataclysmic events, God is doing a work in you and through you. The question is, will you choose to see these events through eyes of faith and hope?

Growth Point 5—Compassionate Service

I beseech you, brethren, (ye know the house of Stephanas, that it is the firstfruits of Achaia, and that they have addicted themselves to the ministry of the saints,)—1 CORINTHIANS 16:15

As every man hath received the gift, even so minister the same one to another, as good stewards of the manifold grace of God.—1 PETER 4:10

For God is not unrighteous to forget your work and labour of love, which ye have shewed toward his name, in that ye have ministered to the saints, and do minister.—HEBREWS 6:10

When you were saved, you were given a gift of service. There's something that God enabled you to do in the local church for the edification and encouragement of others. There's some ability that God has given you for the express purpose of serving Him and magnifying Him.

You weren't designed to be a cul-de-sac Christian—you were created to be a conduit Christian. Grace should flow *through* you, not just *to* you. And few things grow faith like giving out!

Your new nature desires to serve and glorify God. It longs to engage in ministry with Jesus—to co-labor with Him in bringing others into faith and helping them grow. Remember how we talked about "community"? God doesn't merely intend to bring you *into* community with believers, He desires to use you to *bring others into* community!

> *And when Saul was come to Jerusalem, he assayed to join himself to the disciples: but they were all afraid of him, and believed not that he was a disciple. But Barnabas took him, and brought him to the apostles, and declared unto them how he had seen the Lord in the way, and that he had spoken to him, and how he had preached boldly at Damascus in the name of Jesus.*—ACTS 9:26–27

In the verses above, the terrorist Saul (Apostle Paul) had been recently converted to faith in Jesus, but believers didn't believe him. They feared he was setting them up. Thankfully, Barnabas chose to give out and serve. Barnabas chose to engage in personal ministry—to help Saul into the church at Jerusalem and later Antioch. Barnabas expended himself and helped Saul grow in grace with others.

This is God's call to you as well. He calls you from your comfort zone and into real ministry where He can use you to encourage and edify others. As God works in your life, He will open doors of service and opportunities to witness and edify others. He will intersect your path with people whom you can serve.

Your faith will come alive on a new level when you engage in compassionate service. God will change you as He uses you to change others. The most valuable expenditure of your life and resources is people! When you invest into others, you spend your life the way Jesus did.

Growth Point 6—Continual Cultivation

Your heart is a field, and God is the gardener. Your faith has a lot of growing and fruit-bearing ahead. Day by day, God will grow your faith and cultivate fruit if you let Him. This is guaranteed.

One of God's primary instructions to you in His Word is to be patient.

> *For ye have need of patience, that, after ye have done the will of God, ye might receive the promise.*—HEBREWS 10:36

> *Knowing this, that the trying of your faith worketh patience. But let patience have her perfect work, that ye may be perfect and entire, wanting nothing.*—JAMES 1:3–4

> *Be patient therefore, brethren, unto the coming of the Lord. Behold, the husbandman waiteth for the precious fruit of the earth, and hath long patience for it, until he receive the early and latter rain.*—JAMES 5:7

I don't know about you, but I want to grow spiritually mature *right now!* The wait is *killing* me. But in the grand scheme of God's eternal purposes, He's not in a hurry. He could snap His fingers and perfect you instantaneously. For reasons only His heart fully understands, He chooses the slow, lifelong, cultivation method.

Each of the previous five growth points unfolds a gradual work. Settle in. Settle. Your patience and endurance has *"great recompence of reward"* (Hebrews 10:35)! Don't cast away your confidence. Don't get restless in your heart or weary in your mind. You are God's workmanship. He is cultivating you.

Keep yielding. Keep waiting. Keep resting. Continual cultivation is one of the great secrets of real Christianity.

Technology and modern culture offer us instant *everything* in this life—but in God's economy, there is no instant maturity. So settle in for the duration. Hebrews 10 teaches us to draw near to Jesus and hold fast to our faith (Hebrews 10:22–23).

Just keep cultivating!

Six Growth Points of Faith

Six resources are at your disposal—most of them involving His bride, the local church. Think about them, and make a decision as you close this chapter. Decide that no matter where life takes you or what unfolds, you will be found nurturing and cultivating your faith in a healthy local church in these ways:

Growth Point 1—*Communication from the Word*

Growth Point 2—*Community with Believers*

Growth Point 3—*Communion with Jesus*

Growth Point 4—*Cataclysmic Events*

Growth Point 5—*Compassionate Service*

Growth Point 6—*Continual Cultivation*

Faith grows with intention and attention!

Plant yourself in God's greenhouse. Surround yourself with growing believers. Walk personally with Jesus. Let Him grow you through hard stuff. And start investing your life into ministry with Jesus.

Yield yourself in dependence upon Him, and enjoy the journey of growing in God's grace!

For we are labourers together with God: ye are God's husbandry, ye are God's building.—1 CORINTHIANS 3:9

Happy Ending
Keeping the Finish Line in Focus

This past summer, my wife and a visiting friend, Amy, decided to enjoy a day in the outdoors. The summer in New England is beautiful, and Dana told me they planned to go for a drive to see the colonial, Connecticut countryside. It sounded innocent enough, so I wished her well, kissed her goodbye, and dove into a day of study.

It's important to state at this point, that there had been some discussion of a canoe trip down a local river, but the idea was dismissed, at which point I felt it unnecessary to go through my "if you decide to go canoeing" safety spiel. This was a big mistake.

The fact is, while canoeing is a relatively innocuous activity, the local Farmington River does have some small rapids, and these ladies were utterly inexperienced in the art. Had they expressed interest in canoeing, I would have prepared them.

The possibility of their changing their minds never even occurred to me—until the cell phone buzzed at about 4 PM. Time had flown by in my study, and the ladies had been noticeably "out of touch" for several hours.

The phone call was from Dana, and what happened next, I will never forget. I envisioned them at some fruit stand or quiet historic site, as I calmly answered the call. The screaming, frantic voice of my wife exploded from the device...

"Cary, I can't talk long!" She was yelling in desperate and panicked tones. My adrenaline instantly pegged! My heart rushed. My mind raced. *Have they been in an accident, abducted, assaulted, or all three?*

She continued screaming, "We are stuck in the river, our canoe sank, and we are holding on to rocks and tree branches!" She never paused, "They can't find us, but rescuers are looking for us. My battery is almost dead so I can't talk, please help them find us!"

With that she hung up. Seriously—that's all I got, and she was gone. Several seconds of crazy screams, then disconnect. I was mystified. I thought they weren't going canoeing!? Immediately I dialed her back. She answered, again screaming.

"I can't talk, the battery's almost dead..."

"Wait, don't hang up! Are you okay?" I pleaded.

"Yes, we're cold, we're holding on in the middle of the river, and they are looking for us." I pictured rescue boats, helicopters, news choppers hovering over the national forest area. I imagined TV news vans parked along the river. My mind grasped for options. I'm completely removed from the situation. I'm powerless. My wife and her friend are lost, holding on for dear life in a rushing river, and I'm forty-five minutes away with no idea how to help.

"We can't let go of the tree branches because we're afraid of being swept away. The canoe sank. Help them find us! I gotta go, the battery is going to die." And again she hung up.

After a few seconds of gathering my thoughts, I called the canoe shop only to be informed that they didn't know where my wife was, but they were looking.

That's when I remembered the "Find My iPhone" app! Hoping I had enabled Dana's phone, I quickly logged on to the internet, clicked on Dana's phone, and the search began. Within a few seconds, the map opened, and there she was—a blue dot, holding on for dear life in the middle of the Farmington River, invisible from all nearby roads. That was a strange feeling—knowing that blue dot was my desperate wife, but powerless to deliver her.

A few moments later, I texted the screen shot to the rescuers and within about ten minutes, two shoeless, canoe-less ladies climbed up the banks of the Farmington River and began their walk through the woods with their rescuers. A short time later, my wife called. This time her voice was steady and calm. All I could say was, "What in the world?!" Together we laughed as she recounted their last-minute decision to randomly go canoeing—and tell no one!

We laughed with relief that this story had a happy ending.

Seasons of Real Christianity

If there's one thing I'm certain of, it's that the Christian life is seasonal—and some of those seasons are as disorienting and perplexing as my wife and her friend holding on for dear life in a rushing river.

Jesus leads us into seasons of labor and then seasons of rest. He leads us into seasons of testing and then seasons of triumph. Some seasons are abundantly fruitful while others are ominously flat. Sometimes Jesus seems very close while other times He seems distant. Some days you will feel wonderfully victorious; other days you will feel woefully failing.

On some days you will bound out of bed, loving Jesus and ready to serve Him—ready to tell the world of this great Saviour. Other days you won't even want to get out of bed—and it will get worse from there.

At times you will sense God speaking to you through His Word. At other times you will wonder why He's been so silent. Sometimes He will answer your prayers as you hoped. Other times His answer will be "no" or "not now."

If your faith rests on fruit, you're in trouble. If your faith rests in visible results or in sensory experience, you're in bigger trouble. If your faith rests on predictable circumstances or controllable events, your faith will let you down.

If your faith rests in Jesus—it will never fail, because He will never fail!

Real Christianity is a faith journey—which means it's not always visibly measurable or mathematically sensible. It's not always experientially pleasant, but it is always spiritually hopeful!

You won't always know exactly what God is doing or why He's doing it. Quite often, you will scratch your head and wonder, "Jesus, what are You doing?"

His ways are not your ways. His thoughts are not your thoughts. He's not going to explain it all to you. Your questions will not all be answered this side of Heaven. Some seasons will be amazingly life-changing and climactic; other seasons will be boringly redundant and monotonous.

Through it all…

Jesus will never leave you or forsake you.

…for he hath said, I will never leave thee, nor forsake thee.
—HEBREWS 13:5

Jesus will always be with you.

There shall not any man be able to stand before thee all the days of thy life: as I was with Moses, so I will be with thee: I will not fail thee, nor forsake thee.—JOSHUA 1:5

Jesus will help you through every hardship.

When thou passest through the waters, I will be with thee; and through the rivers, they shall not overflow thee: when thou walkest through the fire, thou shalt not be burned; neither shall the flame kindle upon thee.—ISAIAH 43:2

Jesus will give you strength to press on.

Be strong and of a good courage, fear not, nor be afraid of them: for the LORD thy God, he it is that doth go with thee; he will not fail thee, nor forsake thee.—DEUTERONOMY 31:6

Blessed Hope

What if, through all the unpredictable seasons of life, you were sure—absolutely certain—of a happy ending? How would that change your whole life? How would that infuse your heart with hope, even in the hopeless and helpless times.

Real Christianity, more than anything else, is the certain promise of a happy ending with Jesus! It is hope for the heart. It's a blessed hope, a certain hope, a confident hope that rises above every hardship.

It's wonderful to be rescued from sin. It's amazing to be pulled from the treacherous grip of death and placed into the safety of the love of Jesus Christ. It's incredible to walk through this life hand in hand with a Heavenly Father who loves me, protects me, guides me, and comforts me.

But real Christianity is bigger than all that—it's the promise of eternal hope.

The happy ending with Jesus trumps it all! Forever is a very, very long time—longer than our minds can conceive.

But as it is written, Eye hath not seen, nor ear heard, neither have entered into the heart of man, the things which God hath prepared for them that love him.—1 CORINTHIANS 2:9

Every day of your life, God says to your heart, "You haven't seen anything yet!"

God's eternal goodness and everlasting grace have only just begun to be revealed to us. This life is just a shadow—it's like looking through a glass darkly. We can barely begin to imagine the everlasting hope and unfathomable goodness that awaits us in eternity.

> *That in the ages to come he might shew the exceeding riches of his grace in his kindness toward us through Christ Jesus.*—EPHESIANS 2:7

Finishing a Book, Beginning a Journey

I have struggled in writing this book. It's tough to write about truths to which words won't do justice. We've studied some big stuff. There's no way to treat these truths adequately with mere human language.

Ending the book has proved equally challenging. On every page, I've tried to turn your eyes to Jesus—your relationship with Him, your faith in Him, and now your hope in Him. The only way for you to enjoy being a Christian is if you keep your focus on Him and your faith in Him—no matter what.

Men will fail you. Movements will disappoint you. Measurement will discourage you. Jesus will be forever faithful to you.

As you finish this book, you are beginning a wonderful, amazing journey. It's a lifelong walk, a transforming relationship with an unfailing Saviour. The more you know Him, the longer you walk with Him—the more you will love Him and enjoy Him.

If I have given you the impression that I am anything more than a growing, struggling Christian failing my way forward—forgive me. The longer I'm saved, the more aware I am of just how far I have to grow. We are in this struggle together.

To the best of my understanding of walking with Jesus and applying His Word, this is *Real Christianity*. I'm sure my perspective is limited, but together we've discovered these foundational truths about a relationship with Jesus:

- Christianity has been hijacked by religion.
- Jesus is alive, and He is eager to save and change you by His grace.
- Early Christians truly encountered a risen Saviour.
- Christianity is a relationship, not a religion.
- Sin makes me absolutely dependent upon grace.
- Grace is amazing, unconditional, and inexhaustible.
- God loves me *in spite* of me, not *because* of me.
- Jesus accepts me by *birth* not *behavior*.
- I'm not who I *was*, but I'm not who I *will be*.
- Salvation is a three-part miracle—regeneration, renewal, and redemption—and a lifelong process.
- No matter what, God's good work in me goes on.
- Winning is *in* Jesus not *for* Jesus.
- Joyful Christians are repeat offenders, but regular repenters.
- Jesus is someone to run *to*, not *from*.
- Jesus is someone to hide *in*, not *from*
- Faith grows with *intention* and *attention*.
- Blessed hope makes faith worth holding on to.

Real Christians Needed Real Hope

First-century Christians had very hard lives. The American dream hadn't been invented yet. Representative governments didn't exist. Powerful political leaders and powerful religious structures worked hard to extinguish Christianity. Early believers experienced unspeakable pain, bloodshed, and death—just for believing in Jesus.

Throughout the ages, Christianity has rarely had a favorable political climate. To this very day, all over the world, Christians are being tortured, wrongfully imprisoned, and executed by those who hate Jesus and His message. Jesus said this would happen, and He gave us hope.

> *These things I have spoken unto you, that in me ye might have peace. In the world ye shall have tribulation: but be of good cheer; I have overcome the world.*—JOHN 16:33

Much of God's Word encourages Christians to *hold on to hope*, no matter what. Here are just a few places where God addresses eternal hope in temporary hardship:

> *For our light affliction, which is but for a moment, worketh for us a far more exceeding and eternal weight of glory;*—2 CORINTHIANS 4:17

> *Cast not away therefore your confidence, which hath great recompence of reward. For ye have need of patience, that, after ye have done the will of God, ye might receive the promise. For yet a little while, and he that shall come will come, and will not tarry.*—HEBREWS 10:35–37

> *Which hope we have as an anchor of the soul, both sure and stedfast, and which entereth into that within the veil;*—HEBREWS 6:19

> *Looking for that blessed hope, and the glorious appearing of the great God and our Saviour Jesus Christ;*—TITUS 2:13

> *Now our Lord Jesus Christ himself, and God, even our Father, which hath loved us, and hath given us everlasting consolation and good hope through grace, Comfort your hearts, and stablish you in every good word and work.*—2 THESSALONIANS 2:16–17

> *Be patient therefore, brethren, unto the coming of the Lord. Behold, the husbandman waiteth for the precious fruit of the earth, and hath long patience for it, until he receive the early and latter rain. Be ye also*

patient; stablish your hearts: for the coming of the Lord draweth nigh.
—JAMES 5:7–8

In all of these Scriptures, Jesus invites you to hold on to hope—to anchor your soul in Him. When all the world has gone wild—when economies come apart, governments change, and life seems wholly unpredictable and unstable—you have stability in Him. When tragedy unfolds, health gives way, and hardship threatens—you have strength in His grace.

Grace Really Is Amazing

A large portion of this book has been written during an unusually snowy and beautiful New England winter. During these many hours of attempting to write about infinite grace, God has been painting an infinite picture just outside my window.

As I write these words, billions upon billions of white, fluffy flakes are hypnotically floating to their pillowed resting place. It's hard to focus on writing because the abundant snowfall keeps captivating my gaze.

Inside, the fire is warm, and outside the house is enfolded in an endless blanket of white.

When God tried to describe His grace to our finite minds He used snow as His picture: "*...though your sins be as scarlet, they shall be as white as snow...*" (Isaiah 1:18).

Snow. It's His creation and His way of helping my small mind grasp the magnitude of His massive grace. He rains down His grace with more lavish abundance than He rains down snow.

From now until you see Him, He has wrapped you and protected you safely in the vastness of His amazing grace. Every moment of every day He is showering upon you His limitless love, acceptance, and security.

So you can rest. You can absorb the warmth of His love. You can draw near to His heart with full assurance. You can come boldly to His throne.

You can enjoy Him!

When failure seems to be the dominant quality of your real Christian journey, grace is bigger than your failure, and Jesus still carries you forward in love!

Jesus comforted His first followers with these words:

Let not your heart be troubled: ye believe in God, believe also in me. In my Father's house are many mansions: if it were not so, I would have told you. I go to prepare a place for you. And if I go and prepare a place for you, I will come again, and receive you unto myself; that where I am, there ye may be also.—JOHN 14:1–3

You have a blessed hope for a glorious day when all of the struggle will end. That blessed hope makes your faith worth holding on to! Until then, be patient. Endure. Anchor your soul. Stablish your heart. Keep pressing toward the mark. Keep trusting Him. Keep your faith growing in His grace.

Real Christians struggle. They hurt and grow weary. But grace holds them as they hold on to Jesus.

Take hope, friend. Rest in Jesus and His grace. Hold on to your hope! Your "holding on" has a *very happy ending!*

Now the God of hope fill you with all joy and peace in believing, that ye may abound in hope, through the power of the Holy Ghost.
—ROMANS 15:13

About the Author

CARY SCHMIDT has served the Lord for twenty-four years and is the Senior Pastor of Emmanuel Baptist Church of Newington, CT. He is madly in love with his wife of twenty-four years, Dana, and together they have enjoyed raising their three children—Lance, Larry, and Haylee. Cary is first a Christian, husband, and father; second an undeserving pastor of a wonderful church family; and third a writer who enjoys trying to encourage others in their spiritual growth. You can connect with him at caryschmidt.com

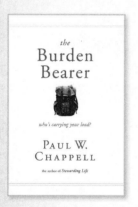
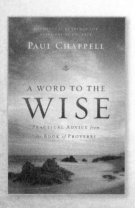

Visit us online

strivingtogether.com

wcbc.edu